FORGING
CHARACTER

Rob Kern

authorHOUSE

AuthorHouse™
1663 Liberty Drive
Bloomington, IN 47403
www.authorhouse.com
Phone: 833-262-8899

Published by AuthorHouse 04/07/2021

ISBN: 978-1-6655-2163-5 (sc)
ISBN: 978-1-6655-2161-1 (hc)
ISBN: 978-1-6655-2162-8 (e)

Library of Congress Control Number: 2021906814

Print information available on the last page.

Bible usage: NIV, ESV, MSG, NLT, NIRV

Dedicated to Ryker and Rylee

Forge within me
A weapon of love
To burn away the parts of me,
And dig up their roots.
The parts of me,
Which grew in with thorns,
Binding the real me.
Create it, O Lord,
And cut me free.

Contents

Chapter 1

SUFFERING AND DESIRE

The Truth of Pain

It was a warm summer evening. I sat in knee deep water, my back against the swimming pool's edge, with my tiny, two-month-old daughter floating blissfully in my arms. Around me, parents, children, and grandparents talked and played and laughed. My little son sloshed around the shallow pool, chasing his friend, with my wife chasing after him. It was a lovely evening made of the stuff of winter's dreams. Summer bliss.

And it was not enough.

Almost foolishly, paradoxically, my heart was heavy with dissatisfaction. I was surprised to find myself lonely - achingly lonely. The cause of the problem seemed indiscernible. It wasn't that I was missing out on conversation - I have that to the brim as a mental health counselor. I did not lack for friends nor family. I felt... missed, or perhaps misunderstood. Like you get when you talk to someone who only half knows you. I wanted to feel known; fully, and completely known. And, in so doing, to better know myself.

I imagined where Jesus might be if he were physically present at the pool. Would he be relaxing on a deck chair with his eyes closed? Standing with the gaggle of other parents watching their children play? Maybe he would be going down the water slide with the youth, whooping on his way down. Would he be seated beside me, resting his back against the edge of the pool? I'd like to think so. That would be lovely - he'd probably know exactly what to say to me, know what my heart needed to hear even if I did not.

That, I decided, was what I was longing for. Jesus incarnate. My creator - the one who knows every intricacy, strength, fear, and desire of my heart - to be there right beside me, to feel the completion of being fully realized by another soul. I longed for perfect intimacy, and felt the acute ache that stemmed from its absence. In the midst of a time when I should have been completely satisfied, my heart wasn't. I'm realizing that it won't ever be. Not until that glorious Day.

It would have been so easy to write off my loneliness and shaken myself out of my dour reverie. I think, in fact, that most of us go about our days living in such a manner. However, more often than not, I find that many unpleasantries are better not left ignored, especially when they seem to crop up out of nowhere and concern matters of the heart. The pain reminds me of the hope I have - the hope all Christians have: that this life, as good as it can be, is not all there is; that our hearts were meant for more, and that more is coming. We are purposed by God to await it, not in despair nor in complacency, but in eager earnestness. The calling is to realize the blessings of the foretastes we receive, but to not be settled by them.

This conundrum serves as one of the primary journeys we all take in life. It is a jarring paradigm shift to put our hope in an invisible God rather than the physical world. The only consistent reminder that we are not where we are meant to be is our uncanny nature to never be satisfied. It is this nature that we either curse, ignore, or learn to live with as a beacon pointing us home.

Suffering

Consider it pure joy, my brothers and sisters, whenever you face trials of many kinds, because you know that the testing of your faith produces perseverance. Let perseverance finish its work so that you may be mature and complete, not lacking anything. - James 1:2-4 NIV

If you're like me, you just glossed over the scripture passages above. It's okay we all have this tendency sometimes. Now, take a look back at it. Notice how it communicates a message that's extraordinarily counter-cultural. The part about not lacking anything sounds pretty nice. But we are supposed to take joy in the trials that test our faith? This ethic doesn't seem fit with our way of being. We're raised to think that if life isn't comfortable, then something is wrong - we must not be doing enough, or doing the right thing. Some of us may even believe that if we are suffering, it's because we're being punished; as though God sees our pain and is happy about it. I cannot imagine anything further from the truth.

David writes this about God in Psalm 56:8 (NLT):

You keep track of all my sorrows.
You have collected all my tears in your bottle.
You have recorded each one in your book.

God knows our every trial. He is near to our pain and suffering. So near, in fact, that he took the punishment that we deserved upon himself through the work Christ accomplished on the cross:

But Christ has rescued us from the curse pronounced by the law. When he was hung on the cross, he took upon himself the curse for our wrongdoing.
- Galatians 3:13 (NLT)

It is pivotal for us to understand that God is not happy about our suffering. He grieves with us when we grieve, suffers with us while we suffer. So why, then, does scripture urge us to delight in our suffering and trials? It seems as though the author of these passages knows something we have forgotten, something that can see us through any adversity: God comes through. Good will suddenly overtake evil. Everything in the gospel, and nearly everything in creation, shouts this truth. New green growth sprouts from the ashes. Planets coalesce from the remnants of supernovas. Spring follows winter. The newborn baby emerges from the pains of birth. And the life Jesus promises comes after death. In Romans 8:18 (NIV), Paul writes:

"I consider that our present sufferings are not worth comparing with the glory that will be revealed in us."

The good that God creates completely outweighs the suffering and brokenness that give way to it. But for now, in this time, and in this life, we *will* face suffering. Jesus guarantees it:

"I have told you these things, so that in me you may have peace. In this world you will have trouble. But take heart! I have overcome the world."
                                                              - John 16:33 NIV

Trouble is going to happen. Arguments, misunderstandings, rejection, betrayals - they are a reality of living in this fallen world. Make no doubt about that. There is perhaps no trouble worse than conflict that drives a relationship apart, particularly where we feel we have a conflict with God. We generally treat conflict with disdain, polarizing ourselves by either avoiding conflict at all costs or constantly picking at it. We look at conflict in our relationships similarly to how we look at suffering: failing to realize that there are opportunities for deeper intimacy through engaging conflict in healthy ways. Conflict has a way of bringing out our innermost and oldest struggles, oftentimes wounds suffered decades ago. But when those past hurts are reopened, oftentimes we only see the surface portion of conflict and fail to address the festering wounds underneath. We don't know what to do with the old scars, so we ignore them and act like we're not living with a limp.

God's offer is that we learn to seize the opportunities presented to us when we become aware of the hurts we carry. Instead of ignoring or being paralyzed by our wounds, we can take our hurts as trailheads leading us towards our healing. Conflict can lead to individual growth as we air our wounds, and relational growth as we come to know others more deeply. If you allow him, God will use conflict to refine you just as he does so with other forms of adversity in your life.

Even the ordinary moments of our lives hold untapped potential for us to mature. But rather than taking advantage of these moments, we spend our lives in either worry and dread, or denial and distraction. We are so resistant to acknowledging our pain that we go so far as to tell others that they can't be in pain either. As a couple's therapist, I oftentimes hear when one spouse complains to the other in the midst of a conflict: "You're always so pessimistic. Why can't you just focus on what's going well?" or "I've already apologized. Can't you move on?" This criticism of the other's pain is about as helpful as telling someone with a broken leg to "walk it off." We cannot simply ignore suffering and think it will go away on its own.

Suffering, problems, pain, conflict... these things must first be addressed if we are to find true peace. Suppressing the pain doesn't heal the wound - we must deal with the actual injury that's causing the pain. But acknowledging our pain and its cause seems like a dangerous thing. We deny our suffering and pretend like we're fine because we fear that the pain will swallow us whole if we bring it into the light. So instead, we give in to the fear and find ways to numb ourselves to it all. However, choosing numbness comes with a tremendous cost. You will not feel desire if you do not allow yourself to also feel suffering, because you will only desire something that you also suffer for. So when we numb ourselves to pain, we end up also numbing ourselves to our dreams. The justification to cut ourselves off from our suffering seems warranted. Even when desires are met, the fulfillment that follows is temporary. While disappointment appears to be inevitable, the problem with numbing ourselves to the pain of disappointment is that it guarantees our perpetual disappointment.

Fear is both the motivation that drives us to avoid suffering, and the product of that avoidance. Fear (the movement away from something unpleasant) is the internal counterpart of hope (the movement towards something wanted). Fear most all works to avoid pain, and thus is prone to either ignore or catastrophize suffering when it is present. Conversely, as we engage our suffering with curiosity, we consequently begin to understand what some of our deepest desires are. For instance, we might suffer from the cruelty of the world and merely fear that we will one day be victim to that cruelty. But if we examine our suffering, we become keen on the fact that we desire something more than what this world offers - a better world, perhaps even our heavenly home. Talking about our pain and unearthing our desires are messy journeys, but I believe that they are better than hiding and allowing our suffering to fester.

Consider a young couple who loses their child during birth. In voicing their pain they discover deep sorrow: the loss of their precious baby, a future they had imagined now stolen, and the futility at all their preparations. But they also find that their pain is directly related to their capacity to love. In other words, if they weren't so loving parents, then their pain wouldn't be so great. They find themselves in a conundrum where their love opens the door to sorrow. Yet despite the pain they are unwilling to forfeit their capacity to love. They would rather hurt and love than not love at all.

Desire enables us to move towards some end or goal *despite* suffering. It propels us to take action towards our dreams even in the face of adversity. However, if our desires are only for the things of this temporary world, we are setting ourselves up for failure. We have to desire something, or *someone*, more permanent and perfect. You see, our desires, however small, reveal an innate longing for God - the only one who is able to satisfy us completely. Every desire within us points to him. Look at how Jesus interacts with a Samaritan woman he meets at Jacob's Well:

> *Jesus answered, "Everyone who drinks this water will be thirsty again, but whoever drinks the water I give him will never thirst. Indeed, the water I give him will become in him a spring of water welling up to eternal life."*
> *- John 4:13-14 NIV*

Jesus takes the woman's desire for water (an earthly, temporary desire) and draws a parallel to desiring God. Water can only stave off thirst for so long, but God fulfills completely. Consider this: if you cut off the suffering associated with being thirsty, then you also eliminate the desire that will compel you to drink. If we numb ourselves to our deepest "thirsts," then we have in part cut ourselves off from desiring Christ, the wellspring of life. No matter what desires we have, we must be aware of how we are contending with the suffering associated with that desire if we are to draw closer to God.

If we only look at our desires as superficial longings for some physical thing, we miss the point. Without allowing our desires to bring us to Christ, we neglect what our hearts truly long for. We drift away from God and find ourselves never truly satisfied. On the other hand, when we search for God in the midst of our desire, we begin the journey of discerning our deepest and truest longings. But this comes with a cost. In order to discover how our desires bring us closer to God, we have to allow ourselves to acknowledge disappointments. Instead of allowing ourselves to be placated by meager crumbs, we must learn to appreciate that our desires will never be fully met on this earth.

In this age of instant gratification, we do not linger in our suffering or desires for very long. We have learned every trick in the book to mitigate our dependency, suffering, and desires. We're hungry so we get fast food. We're lonely so we get on social media. We don't have the answers so we turn to Google. Now, there's nothing inherently wrong with any of those things. The problem is what is going on within our hearts. Pausing to be curious about what our real desires are and how they might best be addressed means patiently enduring suffering, something that instant gratification believes is unacceptable.

Instant gratification reinforces to us that our desires are to be done away with as quickly as possible. Patience and endurance are not options. In the long run, a culture of instant gratification will only perpetuate our angst because it holds no tolerance for disappointment. It teaches us to loathe our suffering, and therefore exacerbates our suffering further.

However, if we were to examine our hearts a little more closely without immediately looking for gratification, we might find a simple fact: the things we're truly, ultimately looking for cannot be found where we're searching. The things of this world might salve our desires for a moment, but completion eludes us. We're barking up the wrong tree. When we come face to face with complex desires that refuse to be immediately gratified, we may begin to recognize that our longings are ultimately meant to draw us into greater intimacy with God. By guarding our hearts to instant gratification and listening to our suffering well, we will be better informed of our desires, which find their fruition in a relationship with Christ characterized by faith. The difficulty will be that the way God fulfills desire is almost always the opposite of instant gratification.

Looking for God in the midst of suffering and desire allows us to grow in intimacy with him, but it means we must learn to be patient. We see God's love and provision even in a glass of water - not merely focusing on the temporary alleviation of our thirst, but yearning for the day when we will thirst no more. This draws us to desire to drink from Christ, and ache for the time when he will fulfill every need we have. Patience teaches us to desire for the fulfillment of God's promise, to the end of suffering where there will be no more need to endure:

And I heard a loud voice from the throne saying, "Now the dwelling of God is with men, and he will live with them. They will be his people, and God himself will be with them and be their God. He will wipe every tear from their eyes. There will be no more death or mourning or crying or pain, for the old order of things has passed away." He who was seated on the throne said, "I am making everything new!"

- Revelation 21:3-5a NIV

This promise is by God's grace alone: that by living in Christ and hoping in God's promises, our suffering takes on an entirely different function. Suffering becomes repurposed - not an indicator that we are failing nor that God is holding out on us, but that we are being strengthened in faith as we await the new order of things. Suffering tells us that we aren't home yet, and becomes the catalyst where we remember to turn our focus on God.

It is a jarring switch to move our gaze from the itch of instant gratification to the anticipation of the final fulfillment of desire, which is found in God. This is the truest desire we have, the thing we are willing to suffer for the most: perfection, complete love, and utter fulfillment. It is the longing to reclaim Eden, to find Heaven, for God to set everything right. And we are entirely dependent on him to make that dream a reality. It can feel easier to focus on immediate gratification - it seems much more in our control. All we can do about God's promises is trust and wait. Faith in God means that we recognize we are entirely dependent on him to fulfill our needs once and for all.

Dependency

Have you ever considered why you have hope and desire in the first place? What function do they serve in our lives? Paul gives us the answer rather bluntly in Romans 8:24 (NIV):

"Who hopes for what they already have?"

Paul is saying that we will not desire or hope for something that we already possess. In other words, we will only want something that we lack.

We become hungry because we lack food in our stomachs. We feel the sensation of thirst because the human body senses when it is dehydrated. Similarly, we are lonely when we lack intimacy and companionship. These predicaments wouldn't exist if we had the ability to be entirely self-sustaining. Indeed, we are incapable of filling those unmet needs by wishing them to be satisfied. If you are dying of thirst, you cannot be truly satiated without actually drinking water, unless by some divine miraculous power. We may choose to ignore the sensation of the need, otherwise known as suffering, but the need will still remain regardless.

We have to look outside of ourselves to meet our inner needs; by ourselves we are incomplete. It is a truth we work ever so hard to nullify. We feign self-sufficiency, oftentimes going so far as to equate our self-worth with our feelings of independence. But this is a fool's errand. Our dependency is a reality we cannot escape despite our efforts to do so. If we could fully provide for ourselves, find every fulfillment of desire internally, then we would have neither desire nor any reason to hope. We would already have everything we need. This obviously isn't the case; we have desire and hope because we are dependent creatures. We must look outside of ourselves for fulfillment, or else give up any hope of fulfillment.

Dependency actually plays a crucial role in our relationship with God, and therefore, our overall health. Christ shows us what our dependent nature is really about:

"Remain in me, as I also remain in you. No branch can bear fruit by itself; it must remain in the vine. Neither can you bear fruit unless you remain in me. I am the vine; you are the branches. If you remain in me and I in you, you will bear much fruit; apart from me you can do nothing."
- John 15:4-5 NIV

If we take Jesus at his word, then the mentality of independence (particularly independence from God) is soul killing. If we cut ourselves off from our support, Jesus tells us that we won't be able to do anything. We will be spiritually dead. What are we to make of life when we strive to become independent, only to find that our independence costs us everything? To truly live, we must embrace our dependency and learn how to connect deeply with God.

Unlike branches, people have a choice of whether or not they will be a part of what gives them life. We can choose to cut ourselves off from God, because God gave us free will. When we turn to Christ, the true vine, the everlasting water, we find life. But we can only come to Christ with our needs when we are willing to be honest that we *are* in need.

The recognition that we are in a state of need is alarming to us. We compulsively take our neediness to all the wrong places: romantic relationships, social praise, addictions, fantasies, and the like. What's more, being unable to independently solve our needs can lead to quite a bit of suffering. Hunger, thirst, and loneliness are painful experiences. But suffering doesn't have to trap us. It can be transformed into desire. Suffering and desire are opposite sides of the same coin. They are different in appearance, but they both stem from the same origin - our dependent nature. You cannot have one without the other. If you feel some measure of desire, you will also feel an amount of suffering.

Some religious traditions believe that desire is the cause of suffering - that if we rid ourselves of desire, then we will be free of suffering. But this is not the case. It is our dependency that creates suffering, not our desires. Ridding yourself of desire will only trap you in misery. Rather, desire is a product of having hope in the face of suffering.

Hope is a crucial aspect of faith, and as such, it begs a closer examination. Hope is not some vague or whimsical feeling. Hope isn't necessarily all warm and fuzzy, either. No, hope is an internal reality we project on the external world which reveals our fundamental beliefs about life and about God. Imagine, for instance, that you put a mouse in a maze. If it has never been in the maze before, it might poke around unsure of what's going on. Eventually the mouse finds the exit and the delicious morsel of cheese waiting for it. You wait a day until the mouse is hungry then put it in the maze again. The mouse remembers the cheese from the day before and quickly sets about running the maze in the hope of alleviating its hunger. In other words, the mouse takes action (running the maze), prompted out of a combination of suffering (hunger), desire (cheese), and hope (belief that the cheese can be obtained by running the maze).

Similarly, imagine a person stranded in a desert. The sun-beat dunes all around them do not bear the life-giving sight of an oasis. The person knows it's only a matter of time until they will die of thirst. At first, they are eager and full of hope. Maybe there will be a stream beyond the next rise. As they traverse deeper and deeper into the desert, however, hope begins to run thin. The hours start mounting up, their feet blistering and their mouth is now dry and cracked. They doubt there will be anything good over the next hill. And why shouldn't they doubt? There hasn't been any sign of relief so far! Yet even the faintest murmur of hope will keep them going. Until they finally see it - the oasis. They run to it, and as they near, the sight shimmers away into the hot, quivering air. A mirage. They stand over the spot, trying to will the oasis back into reality, but to no avail. Their knees start giving out. Now comes the final test: will they give up hope and lie down in the sand to await death, or will the slim chance that water *just might* be over the next dune be enough to draw them once again to their feet? Never underestimate hope. It might be the thing that compels us forward, but, when misplaced, hope can also drive us mad.

All that to say: if we have hope, then our desires compel us to take action. Desire is a movement towards some positive outcome related to whatever it is we are hoping for. When I'm hungry, I typically don't complain about the suffering of my hunger. Instead, because I have hope, I say I want to go get lunch. I have this hope because of my repeated experiences of dealing with my dependent need for food. I have learned that my hunger is not a harbinger of doom, but a need that can be met through various means I get to choose between. But even if we do have desire, there isn't a guarantee that we will move forward with hope. We might find ourselves paralyzed by desire's evil twin: fear.

Fear and Desire

Let's compare desire and fear to a computer's operating system. An operating system is pervasive, forming the context of everything else that happens when a computer is operating. It hosts nearly all the functions that the computer user will utilize. If you were to change an operating system, you'd change almost everything about the computer: different programs, different data, different means of storage, and different user interfacing. So, while different operating systems can fulfill the same role, they perform in entirely different ways. The same is true of desire and fear. When they take root in us they become the core means of how we operate, influencing everything else we think, feel, say, and do.

Fear and desire are laborious to tell apart, like a shirt you can't tell whether it is inside-out or rightside-in until you find the faded, barely-there tag. Telling one from the other takes a healthy amount of persistence, self-awareness, and a willingness to deeply examine the motivations that drive us.

For example, one time I had a conversation with a colleague where we discussed the subtle distinctions between true acceptance and denial masquerading as acceptance. After the loss of a loved one, for instance, one person might say that they have accepted the loss and are trying their best to move forward in life. But another person says they have accepted it, *thank you for asking*.

With near identical language, the former appears to have truly dealt with the loss where the latter is eager to talk about something else. But what if the opposite were true? What if the former only feigns composure to politely distract where the latter is truly thankful that someone is talking to them about their loss? As you can see, we need more information than words alone can convey. To tell acceptance and denial apart we need to know the person in question, we need to hear their tone and inflection, and to see their body language. We need to listen with our ears, eyes, and our gut. The same applies to telling apart fear and desire.

What, then, are we listening for? What distinguishes desire from fear? Fear manifests as avoidance, a movement *away* from something perceived as negative. It might be the avoidance of a particular topic, situation, or outcome. Oftentimes I can discern someone's fear when their desires appear in the negative form - when someone says what they do *not* want. They might say something like: "I don't want people to judge me." They fear negative judgment and possibly rejection. Fear is a problematic operating system because it can never reach any kind of definitive goal or objective. While fear avoids, desire moves towards some objective in a tangible way. Desire can have its goals met, as it states specifically what the objective is. Desire might say: "I want to be accepted."

The difference between fear and desire might not seem all that great until we consider how each of them responds to the same situation. When the fear of judgment and the desire for acceptance each attend a social gathering, the results are quite different. The fear would be paranoid that people might be secretly criticizing them, that although others seem to be laughing their only faking it, or that once they leave the others will talk about them behind their back. On the other hand, desire finds the fulfillment of their hope and enjoys it. Even in the worst case scenario, if the social gathering was a negative experience, fear and desire still produce different results. Fear would take the pain as confirmation that they were right to be afraid, and compel the person to further isolate themselves. Desire looks at failure as a means to learn and do something different next time, such as hanging out with different people. We can let fear paralyze us and prevent us from reaching our objectives, or we can choose to live in desire by examining our motives and deepest dreams.

Human beings feel suffering because we are unable, in and of ourselves, to meet our own longings. I cannot wish my dependency away. We must look outside of ourselves in order to satiate our internal desires. Hence why desire, which compels us towards an objective, is so imperative. Where fear stops us in our tracks, desire opens the door to the possibilities within our reach. When the raw signals of suffering are reframed as desires with hope, we begin to search for fulfillment. Here's an example of the entire process at work:

It has been several hours since I have eaten. My stomach has digested my last meal, and senses that it is lacking sustenance. So my stomach sends a neural message to my brain, which I experience as hunger. I experience the sensation of hunger as a kind of suffering. I don't enjoy the feeling, but I can't make it go away without doing something about it, nor can I afford to ignore it. If I leave my hunger unaddressed by trying to suppress the discomfort, my state will worsen as I begin to experience starvation. So I must do something. Luckily, I believe that I can realistically address the problem. I have hope because I remember that there are leftovers in the fridge, and plenty of other options if my leftovers have gone bad. The suffering of my hunger, therefore, becomes translated into desire. This desire compels me to take certain action. In this case, I get off my computer and start rummaging around for the leftovers. I heat my food up in the microwave, find a fork, and get to eating. This temporarily resolves my dependent need for food and the associated discomfort of hunger. In conclusion, my lack of sustenance, felt as the pain of hunger, combined with the hope available food, became a desire for lunch, which compelled me to take action to find momentary fulfillment. All for a plate of spaghetti.

Although we can take personal action to find fulfillment, we are absolutely dependent on outside influence. Fulfillment requires the participation of both ourselves and an outside influence - we have to do something about our suffering, yet we are also reliant upon external forces. This fact remains true even for spiritual matters. We need God to come through, but we must also come to God. This lack of complete control fosters fear where we have not learned to do our part and trust God with the rest. Like your health, you can control certain things about what you do, such as what you consume, whether you exercise, and how often you visit your doctor. But there are forces beyond your control. Despite your best efforts, you may contract some disease. Fear focuses on the dreaded, uncertain factors beyond our control, while desire concerns itself with what is both within our control and realistically attainable.

We have a choice of whether or not to take personal action to find fulfillment. In addition, we also choose whether we will involve others in our search for fulfillment. The interaction between our personal movement towards fulfillment and the involvement of an outside influence has profound effects on our character, leading us to either faith, manipulation, greed, or apathy. Faith operates when we put our hope in God, in the midst of desire, in the face of disappointment, without trying to control the outcome. Manipulation demands that others fulfill our needs while we do relatively little. Greed excludes others from our search for fulfillment and only relies on selfishness. And finally, Apathy neither compels us to do anything to find personal fulfillment, nor allows others to help us do so; Apathy gives up desire to resignation. It is my firm conviction that it is *only* through Faith that genuine fulfillment can be obtained.

We can seemingly find gratification without Faith, but the problem is that the gratification becomes ruined by the process we took to obtain it. Only Faith allows us to enjoy the results of our search without a taint of guilt or regret. For instance, I might enjoy going out to dinner with my friends when I know they have also chosen to be there. But if I were to manipulatively force them to come, greedily eat dinner on my own, or apathetically pretend like I never wanted to go out for dinner at all, then the meal isn't as good. We have a paradox, then: *how* you reach fulfillment has more influence upon your satisfaction than *whether* you find fulfillment. In other words, it is better to have had faith and been disappointed than it is to have found gratification by any means necessary.

Let's look at a graphic that demonstrates this process. This model will form the backbone for us to examine the interplay between our relationships and our desires:

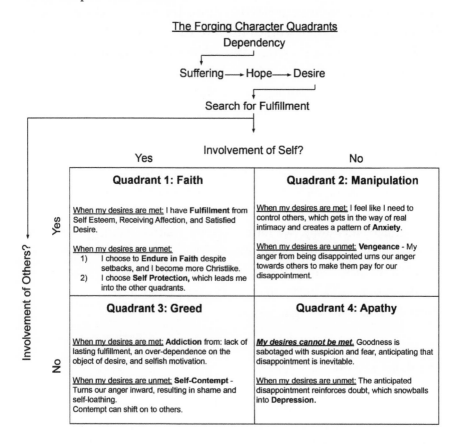

Our dependent nature means that we will, at times, lack something essential to our being. This state of need is felt as suffering to some extent or another - beginning with discomfort and mounting to agony, should the need go unaddressed. When we have hope, we move our focus from the pain of our suffering to the object of our desire, our goal. Desire compels us to search for some means of fulfillment. We choose whether or not we will act with personal volition and whether or not we will allow others to play a part in our fulfillment. The interaction of these choices produces the four quadrants of Faith, Manipulation, Greed, and Apathy.

As you can see, fulfillment can only be found when desires are met in the quadrant of Faith, where the means is greater than the ends. Even when the other quadrants obtain their desires, fulfillment is not experienced. Now, if genuine fulfillment is truly only experienced in the quadrant of Faith, then why doesn't everyone do it? To put it simply, it is because there are tremendous risks involved in Faith. There is a real potential to be disappointed, rejected, or scorned when you are open. Faith is vulnerable.

Many of us make ourselves vulnerable without knowing it. We are ignorant of the risks we are taking, and thus, in bliss. But when some harm befalls us when we are vulnerable, we shirk back. We're like Adam and Eve after they've eaten the forbidden fruit, suddenly our eyes are open to our vulnerability. This newfound awareness comes at a tremendous cost. It becomes more difficult to operate from a position of love when we are anxious of what vulnerability might cost us. When disappointment and rejection seem to become the overwhelming realities in our lives, we lose heart. So, in a desperate attempt to salvage ourselves, we change tactics and push vulnerability away. We forfeit love for control, selfish gratification, or the supposed security of numbness. These forces do not give us the salvation we seek. Rather, they trap us in cycles of insecurity, addiction, and depression. What are we to make of our longings and our relationships when the stakes are so high?

The Risks of Faith

The quadrant of Faith examines how we manage our desires and relationships with honesty and openness, aka, vulnerability. Finding fulfillment through Faith is all at once an empowering and sobering experience. We recognize our own courage at taking the leap, we are humbled by others' goodwill towards us, and grateful to have our desires met. On the other hand, when we are vulnerable and then disappointed or rejected we can be left feeling disillusioned, bitter, and resentful. Living in Faith presents a dichotomy that is difficult to resolve.

It is not enough to be left alone with our newfound awareness of vulnerability, lest we come to despise vulnerability. We must also learn to have mastery of our vulnerability, of our Faith. Mastery will not mitigate the risks associated with Faith, only help us to move forward in Faith with confidence and wisdom.

For example, consider an innocent child who wants to make a new friend. Ignorant of their vulnerability, the child invites another kid to come play. When the child is rejected and called names like "weird" or "stupid," they are obviously hurt. They still want a friend, but are now wary of approaching others. Before asking another kid to play, they flashback to the prior rejection and squash their desire. The awareness of their vulnerability seemingly makes matters worse. One day, the child somehow learns to accept that not everyone will want to play, and that they cannot control what others think of them. They are fully aware that when they ask someone to play, they might get rejected. Only now they are equipped to deal with the rejection. They are back to asking, having wisened up to the dangers that asking comes with.

Awareness of our vulnerability means that we know our desires and relationships poise us to either experience intimacy and satisfaction, or isolation and disappointment. That awareness might be painful, but now that we are aware of our vulnerability, we can do something with it. Oftentimes we scorn vulnerability simply because we do not know how to manage the disappointment we have either experienced in the past or imagined in the future. We don't know what to do with the pain, so we push it away. Anyone can handle fulfillment well. Little is revealed of our character when life always goes our way. It is in unfulfilled, dejected desire where our character is forged.

By acknowledging our pain we become aware of our vulnerability. What we are then lacking is healing that frees us to be both vulnerable and strong. It is impossible to step forward vulnerably while we are simultaneously working to cover up where we've been hurt before. We're going to need more than a band-aid.

Faith requires healing.

Healing means that your wounds will be exposed.

The exposure of your wounds is a tremendous risk, perhaps the riskiest aspect of Faith.

In order to heal we have to unlearn the ways we have suppressed our wounds and acted like we're invulnerable. Awareness goes a long way to help in this regard, but then we are invited to do something terrifying: to allow God into the midst of our past and current pain, disappointment, and vulnerability. Fear will undoubtedly crop up in an attempt to protect you from your wounds. That's understandable. Fear is like your soul's equivalent to the body's pain system. Just like any physical wound, healing the soul wound won't be comfortable, but it will be good.

Making use of our awareness, pursuing healing means examining ourselves, the others around us, and our surroundings. We pay attention to where and how we were hurt in the midst of our most vulnerable moments, and invite God into the wound so that he can heal it. Those moments are sacred. We typically only share the stories of our wounds with those we trust the most, and so a trusting relationship with God is a prerequisite. This is a personal journey not to be taken lightly or quickly. Remember, the goal is deep, personal healing, not a band-aid.

As we are healed, we find that our vulnerable desires are no longer bound to merely fulfillment or disappointment. There now exists a third outcome where our desires aren't met as we'd prefer but we have learned to live well despite it. It reminds me of a cultural proverb I once heard: If you want to hear "yes," you have to be willing to hear a lot of "no." Our ability to endure rejection and disappointment grows, and therein our capacity for Faith grows. Our character is strengthened as a result of choosing to embrace our vulnerability, showing that we care about something more than our immediate comfort.

On the other hand, when we encounter disappointment yet continue to insist that our desires *must* be met, we resort to Greed and/or Manipulation. Greed and Manipulation seek to guarantee gratification by either eliminating the involvement of others or controlling what others do. When even those tactics fail us, we are driven to hopeless Apathy, where we rid ourselves of desire in a desperate attempt to also be rid of suffering.

Apathy means "a loss of will or motivation," which I believe equates to a complete loss, or death, of desire. Think of it this way: desires exist because we are lacking something and hoping for fulfillment. Without hope, desire becomes an awful thing, something to be done away with, an enemy. So, we kill our desires in an attempt to plug up our suffering. Perhaps we feel the sting of loneliness, and we have learned that neither Manipulation nor

Greed satiates our loneliness, and so we resolve to eliminate any need we have for relationship. As a result, Apathy seals our fate - we construct our own prison, staving off any hope of fulfillment.

No one immediately defaults to Apathy, however. It is a slow decline, beginning with disappointment, growing into doubt, and aided by our mishandling of desire through Manipulation and Greed. Living with our desires is one of the biggest risks that we can take, and how we resolve that risk dictates our character, compelling us to become people of Faith, Manipulation, Greed, or Apathy.

In James 4:1-3, the author observes how some people try to resolve their desires:

"What causes fights and quarrels among you? Don't they come from your desires that battle within you? You want something but don't get it. You kill and covet, but you cannot have what you want. You quarrel and fight. You do not have, because you do not ask God. When you ask, you do not receive, because you ask with wrong motives, that you may spend what you get on your pleasures."

- James 4:1-3 NIV

I believe that James is noting the distinction between Faith, Manipulation, and Greed. Strife, which James calls fighting and quarreling, comes from idolizing oneself by prioritizing the gratification of our desires above all else. Manipulation and Greed are the products of this idolatry, and would rather mistreat others if it meant they could find personal fulfillment. Faith, on the other hand, prioritizes love above the gratification of one's desires. James even says that when we do ask, our hearts must be in the right place. God will not be manipulated by those who feign to have faith but are only out for their own gratification. Through Faith, asking is not motivated by selfish fulfillment, but becomes the context to build trust and love in a relationship with another person regardless of the gratification of our desires.

Faith handles desire far differently than any of the other quadrants. In Faith, we accept that others have the freedom to choose whether or not they will act as we desire. Faith understands that desire is part of what it means to be dependent, and not the cause of suffering. Faith acknowledges that fulfillment isn't obtained through self-sufficiency or control, but instead through the delight of intimacy in the process of trusting. In the book, *The Truce of God*, Rowan Williams describes the distinction between "pure desire" and "impure desire," with I believe to be the difference between Faith and its alternatives:

"Pure desire is desire that longs to grow endlessly in knowledge of and rootedness in reality and truth. Impure desire desires to stop having to desire, to stop needing; it asks for a state where, finally, the ego can relax into self-sufficiency and does not have to go stuffing bits and pieces of the world into itself in order to survive. Real desire can live with an unlimited horizon - which religious people call God - while unreal desire stumbles from moment to moment trying to gratify an immediate hunger, without accepting that 'hunger' is part of being human and so cannot be dealt with or understood by an endless succession of leak-plugging operations."[1]

Our limitless "hunger" is our desire for an infinite God, nothing else. Seen through this light, our ache for fulfillment can either help us to understand ourselves, or drives us to try to eliminate our desires entirely. Faith understands that living with desire is part of what it means to be human and so looks for fulfillment greater than instant gratification. Desire that draws us to truth and to God compels us towards Faith, but desire that demands gratification and self-sufficiency causes us to stray elsewhere.

Dear friends, I urge you, as foreigners and exiles, to abstain from sinful desires, which wage war against your soul.
- 1 Peter 2:11 NIV

Fear that seeks to eliminate desire and vulnerability, the striving for self-sufficiency, sets us up for failure. We cannot be rid of desire, and therefore, these sinful desires wage war against our core nature - our very souls. Pure desires, on the other hand, present us with opportunities to come before God in eager expectation:

Give ear to my words, O LORD, consider my sighing. Listen to my cry for help, my King and my God, for to you I pray. In the morning, LORD, you hear my voice; in the morning I lay my requests before you and wait expectantly.
- Psalm 5:1-3 NIV

Notice that in the above verses the author is quite bold in their hope to have their requests fulfilled. I believe this boldness comes from a heart that is more concerned with being heard by God and obeying him than having God do exactly what is asked of him. This is Faith at work: the prioritization of the quality of the relationship above selfishness; a preference to be disappointed if it means being connected, believing that the connection itself brings more satisfaction than instant gratification. Faith is clinging to God while acknowledging our desires and vulnerabilities. Evil works together to try to kill our desires by compelling us to curse our seemingly unmanageable longings. Where we don't have desire, we have no need for Faith.

Do your desires lead you towards a real relationship with God, or do they war against your soul, driving you further from him? When we learn to turn towards God in Faith rather than solely looking for him to meet our desires, we begin to recognize that the true fulfillment we long for is a real relationship with God. That relationship allows us to build trust in God even in the midst of disappointment.

In order to do this, however, we must learn how to handle momentary disappointment without losing Faith. The ability to maintain hope despite disappointment is the defining moment of Faith. This perseverance comes unnatural to everything our intuition seems to tell us. If others let us down, we consider it to be normal when we begin to distrust them. But God asks us to do the opposite: to maintain our Faith in him by trusting him even when it doesn't make sense to us.

Faith is hard, but God is faithful. His pursuit of us is unfailing, but this does not mean that he will immediately gratify each and every inkling of desire that we have. God makes it clear that our desires' primary purpose is to bring relational fulfillment in him, not transitory fulfillment in having our desires quenched. We build trust with God by allowing our desires to turn us towards Faith in him, setting our hope in his promises even if we cannot foresee their fruition. Faith builds our resiliency to handle disappointment without becoming embittered. Where disappointment used to leave us empty and broken, it now provides a far deeper satisfaction - life lived with God.

As human beings we are hardwired to avoid pain, and this can cause us to resist acknowledging our pain, vulnerability, and unmet desires. But as Christians we know that being honest about our suffering is a catalyst that matures us and brings us closer to God. Crabb et al. wrote about this crucible in the book, *Men of Courage*, as they envisioned what it would be like if more Christians decided to engage the difficulties in life they otherwise shrink from:

"If I look hard into my dream, I can see an army of wise men and women distributed among God's people, armed only with gentle discernment and penetrating wisdom, character qualities that have been forged in the fires of suffering."[2]

The qualities of discernment and wisdom, gained from having endured in Faith, represent only a fraction of the characteristics God matures within us. These positive qualities are certainly far departures from the pitfalls of Manipulation, Greed, and Apathy. And yet, these positive character values are not the ultimate goal. Refining our character isn't about developing values, it's about an intimate relationship with God that can endure through anything. Being confident in vulnerability doesn't just magically happen, it comes from having an unshakeable place of security - our trust in God.

The Forging Character Quadrants

Let's review what we've established so far. (It may be worth bookmarking the chart depicted earlier.) We began with the notion that human beings are dependent entities - requiring outside influence in order to even survive. We need things like food, water, air, shelter, and relationships. Our dependency predisposes us to be in a state of need and we find that we cannot satiate ourselves independently. This creates the experience of suffering, which is the awareness of an unmet need to a varying degree of severity. If we have hope, suffering becomes translated into desire, which is the force which motivates us to seek fulfillment. As we search for fulfillment, we ultimately have only two factors that we may utilize: we can decide to take personal action or not, and we also choose whether or not to involve others. The interaction between the involvement of oneself and others gives us the four quadrants of Faith, Manipulation, Greed, and Apathy.

These quadrants describe the kinds of tactics by which we live, and come to determine our character. We will now examine each of the Forging Character Quadrants in greater detail, shedding light on how they are characterized, what happens when they find gratification, and how they react to disappointment.

Verse to remember: Not only so, but we also glory in our sufferings, because we know that suffering produces perseverance; perseverance, character; and character, hope. And hope does not put us to shame, because God has poured out his love into our hearts by the Holy Spirit, whom he has given us. Romans 5:3-5

Thought to consider: Manipulation, Greed, and Apathy are forces of mistrust that hinder us from experiencing pure desire and authentic relationships, which encourage our relationship with God.

Questions to ponder:

- How do you respond to disappointment?
- What desire do you have difficulty trusting God with?
- What are the risks of Faith?

Note to the Reader: Faith denoted by an upper-case "F" will refer to the Forging Character Quadrant of Faith, whereas a lower-case "f" will be used to talk about faith in the usual sense.

Chapter 2

FAITH

Now faith is confidence in what we hope for and assurance about what we do not see.

- Hebrews 11:1 NIV

The Whipper of Faith

A few years ago I became certified to lead climb in an indoor rock climbing gym. Lead climbing is a bit different than your average experience rock climbing. Traditional "top-rope" climbing involves moving up the wall while being connected via your climbing rope through an anchor at the top of the wall, and then back down to a belayer on the ground. If you lose your grip while top-roping, you typically only fall a few feet at most.

Lead climbing is an altogether different beast. When lead climbing, you tie the rope directly to your harness and connect straight to the belayer, without being secured to the climbing wall in any way. As you climb, you take the rope up with you while your belayer lets out slack. While you move up the wall you have to clip the rope through anchor points set into the wall. What this means, in essence, is that you have to climb *above* the point where your rope passes through an anchor in the wall. When you fall from above your last anchor point, you drop (at the least) to the anchor plus the equivalent of any slack that was in the rope before you fell. If you fall from 10 feet above your anchor, you'll fall a total of roughly 20 feet. All that momentum usually means that your belayer is going to get launched off the ground, which usually adds extra distance to the fall. This kind of fall is called a "Whipper" and is one of the most dangerous (and fun) aspects of climbing.

To be cleared to climb I had to demonstrate competency in all the required skills. This culminated in ascending a wall three stories tall and purposely falling from above my anchor point. Now, I'd like to think of myself as a relatively courageous person. I'm no adrenaline junkie, but when I set my mind to do something, I want to see it through. But that day, clinging with a sweaty grip to the top of that wall, I froze.

The call came from below that they were ready for me to fall. But my thoughts wandered. I had never taken a whipper from this high before. I could feel the height in my gut. I thought to let go, but my hands refused to obey. I closed my eyes. I told myself to let go on the count of 3, but when the countdown ended I was still hanging on. I started to panic, and the countless things that could go wrong flashed through my mind in an instant. Did I tie my knot right? Is my harness strong enough to take this fall? What if my anchor rips free of the wall? Will my belayer catch me?

By this point, I thought the others below were undoubtedly watching me and wondering what I was doing. I felt shame for holding on so long, frozen with fear. It was one of those moments that was only a few seconds, but felt like it could have been hours. Then I made the rookie mistake - I looked down. "I could hit the ground," said the fear in my head. "The ground padding is too thin. A fall from this high and I'll be dead. I could die. Even if I live, I'll be mangled, broken, and wracked with pain."

Then, unexpectedly, a different inner voice spoke: "Do I accept that risk?" After a moment of inner wrestling, I thought: "Yes," and my hands finally popped off the wall. I felt my stomach lurch at the sudden drop. The whipper started as a free-fall, and all sense of control vanished. I passed my anchor and kept falling. Finally I felt the glorious tug of tension on my rope and swung in gently towards the rock wall. About at that moment, the joy of the thrill hit me. By the time my belayer began to lower me, I found I was actually sad to come down! Something in me instantly wanted to recreate that moment. Even to this day, when I climb I try to recapture those moments of surreal abandon, but they're harder to hold onto than any rock wall.

Scripture talks about faith, hope, and love as pinnacle qualities (1 Corinthians 13:13), but I think that faith is probably the hardest thing to have in the world. Without the work of the Spirit, I'm convinced faith would be impossible. Personally, I'm more comfortable with the notion of love. Even hope is pleasant - the anticipation that something good is coming. But faith... faith requires something more than warm, fuzzy feelings.

Ever since I've been a boy I've been enamoured with climbing. My favorite thing to climb was the highest pine tree in our backyard, which was taller than our two-story home. I spent my summers clearing out the interior of that pine tree, breaking off pokey sticks so that I had a clear path to the top. And there I would sit, looking down over our neighborhood. When the wind blew, I'd hear it whistle through the needles and I'd gently sway with the tree. I'm sure I gave my mother a heart attack!

Love is what compels me to climb. Hope, on the other hand, is envisioning the goodness of the climb. Hope imagines the thrill of reaching the top of those branches and anticipating the fulfillment I feel when I make it back down safely. But my love and hope can be quite naive at times. They don't take any consideration about the danger of perching atop thin branches some thirty feet in the air.

Not so with Faith. It is anything *but* naive. Faith looks danger in the eye. It sees all the potential risks, consequences, and rewards. Yet, despite the danger, Faith chooses to climb. Faith is trusting the branches and my climbing ability combined with the recognition and acceptance that something could go wrong and send me plummeting to the ground below. Faith is belief in the security of what we rely upon in spite of our knowledge of danger. It can seem much easier to simply stay on the ground rather than coming face to face with the risks inherent to Faith.

Made for Faith

Faith requires us to be courageously vulnerable. At first glance, it seems safer to turn away from situations that require us to have Faith. We ignore our mortality, oftentimes focusing on creature comforts that we believe we are entitled to and are within our control. Why would we put ourselves in situations that demand we confront risk, and trust in something besides ourselves? Rock climbing seems a foolhardy risk compared to the safety of our own two feet on the ground. Survival-mechanisms within us prompt us to run from danger, to not relying on anyone or anything else. The problem is that Faith is dangerous, but we cannot afford to run from Faith forever. Running away from Faith sucks the life out of us. We forget that the ground is not as solid as we think - just ask anyone who has lived through a serious earthquake. You cannot run from every danger, because "safety" is a misnomer. Nothing is safe. To be alive is to live side by side with danger, and thinking otherwise is only denial. Even if avoiding every danger were possible, it may keep you alive, but it cannot give you real *life*.

There's a quote I keep on my office door that reads:

"A ship in harbor is safe -- but that is not what ships are built for."[1]
- John A. Shedd

Just as our bodies will atrophy if left to the safety of idle comfort for too long, so too will our hearts wither if we do not face the rough seas of Faith. But we hesitate to live in Faith because it seems too risky, too vulnerable. Indeed, we are caught between two difficulties: to live an isolated, self-protected life; or to live in Faith and risk the potential of being hurt. If we're being honest with ourselves, we can acknowledge that both pathways are dangerous. So which are we to choose? The danger of risk or the danger of boredom? Faith or Apathy?

If you had never seen a ship before, or didn't know the reason for which it was built, it would be easy to misunderstand its purpose. You might think it was meant to simply dock at harbor indefinitely. Similarly, we must know the purpose we were built for. We can definitively say that God made us for Faith because of the creation narrative found in Genesis chapters 1-3. These chapters reveal insight about the nature of mankind. We are meant to live in enduring relationships through Faith. We thrive in risk rather than in protected isolation because we weren't made to be hidden away or isolated. God created Adam and Eve to know them, and for them to know one another completely and feel no shame.

In Genesis 1:26 God created mankind in his own image, male and female, to have dominion over the Earth and all the living creatures in it.

Crabb et al. observe in the book, *Men of Courage*[2] that Adam carries the image of the Creator by cultivating order from chaos. Just as God created the Earth by organizing form from disorderly darkness, so too is Adam meant to create order from chaos. This even carries into how Adam was created: God formed him from the dust of the ground from *outside* of Eden, where things were more messy. After God created Adam, he then took him to Eden to tend to the garden (Genesis 2:15). Adam is told that he is free to eat from any tree in the Garden. The only stipulation is that Adam is not to eat from the Tree of the Knowledge of Good and Evil, lest he die.

What do you suppose Adam made of this command? Surely he must take God at his word. We do not see Adam immediately saunter off, doubting the seriousness of the command and finding out *for himself* if God's command can be trusted. God begins his relationship with mankind in trust. From what we can infer, God leaves the Tree of Knowledge in the middle of the Garden, right out in the open. The only thing keeping Adam away from it is his continual choice to trust God.

At this point in the creation story, God declares that everything is "good." Everything so far is going according to plan. Yet, after Adam is placed in Eden and given the command not to eat from the Tree of Knowledge, God makes an observation:

"It is not good *that the man should be alone, I will make him a helper fit for him."*

- *Genesis 2:18 (ESV, emphasis added)*

Although Adam is with God in the Garden of Eden, God says that Adam is "alone." God recognizes that Adam lacks an equal partner. This gap in creation is the first thing that God says is "not good." Remember back to the Forging Character Quadrants that it is in the state of need where suffering abounds. Adam was created to reflect the nature of the three-in-one God, who exists in perfect relationship with himself. As such, without an intimate human relationship, Adam is in a state of discontent. The first observable desire of mankind, the desire for human relationship, becomes apparent in the absence of Eve.

Consider what would have happened if God had chosen to do nothing - if he hadn't created Eve. Adam would have been aware of some longing he couldn't place. Perhaps he would feel the discontent more sharply when seeing animals in their pairs. He would have felt the sting of loneliness in Eve's absence, and experienced suffering from a lack of fulfillment, perhaps without even knowing what it was he was missing. And there would've been nothing Adam could have done about it. The absence of Eve is not something Adam can fix. He needs God to come through. God does indeed solve Adam's loneliness, but not in the way we might expect. Instead of immediately creating Eve and nipping the problem in the bud (remember, this is before the Fall), God gives Adam a job. He is to name the animals and seemingly search for his partner, the solution to his loneliness, from among them.

Let's pause for a moment to consider how this story is unfolding. Adam feels the sting of loneliness, so God has him look through the animals to find his partner. God takes a situation that is undoubtedly difficult for Adam, and makes it worse by asking him to perform a task he knows Adam is doomed to fail. It's absurd! We the audience know that Adam needs Eve, yet God occupies him with an aggravating and time-wasting task.

Have you ever wondered why?

Yet, Adam appears to jump right into the task. Adam entrusts his desire for a suitable helper to God, and God initially responds in a way that is anything but instantly gratifying. Scripture tells us that Adam made it through all the birds, livestock, and beasts. ALL. OF. THEM. And what was the result of Adam's efforts?

But for Adam no suitable helper was found."

- Genesis 2:20b NIV

Is this how we would expect God to respond to pre-fall Adam's suffering? How are we to make sense of this story?

God reminds me of a parent on Christmas morning, teasing Adam as he eyes his presents under the tree. "Oh, you want to open your presents? Hold on, let me go get some coffee. Why don't you count the presents until I get back, and see if there's one that you especially want to open. Just wait a while longer." Only once Adam starts opening his presents, he finds that all of them are empty. What then? Perhaps Adam will rant and rage, or throw his hands up and storm back to his room. No, I imagine Adam looking at God, squinting suspiciously, knowing God must have something else up his sleeve. "Oh, they're all empty? Huh that's strange. Wait, Adam, why don't you come out to the garage with me?" And there it waits: the big, wrapped box with the red bow.

God's actions here suggest that he cares about something more than the gratification of desire or alleviating discomfort. God moves Adam into a situation where his Faith will be tested. Adam had to make a choice. Trust God, or don't trust God. And thus, Adam's character is revealed.

At being given his task, Adam could have thrown a fit and complained that his needs were not being met. Perhaps he could have tried to bargain with God, offering to name the animals *after* God dealt with his loneliness. Yet, from what we observe in scripture, Adam simply does his job. I wonder if Adam felt frustrated when he was repeatedly disappointed:

"Cheetah… No."

"Groundhog… Not that one."

"Wolf… Almost?"

"Pigeon… Next."

I wonder if the animals were paraded before Adam, Noah's Ark style, or whether he had to go and scour the Earth for them all. God bringing the animals to Adam could mean a lot of different things. Either way, I imagine it took eons to go through just the birds, let alone "all the livestock (…) and beasts of the field," (Gen 2:20a). Adam sticks it out despite three major setbacks: God gives him a job instead of immediate gratification, he faces countless disappointments along the way, and his final effort fails to produce a suitable helper. What surely felt like an endless task must have left him disappointed - he failed to find what he was looking for. Just as when you're hungry and don't find anything in your fridge to eat, Adam was surely even more keenly aware of his desire for companionship after his efforts proved fruitless. But Adam's hope and trust in God appears unshaken. Adam is more committed to maintaining his Faith in God than he is to his own gratification.

Can you imagine what would have happened if Adam had given up - if his frustration had gotten the better of him? If Adam hastily rushes into trying to learn a "lesson" prematurely he'll miss the point. If he resorts to Manipulation, he'll try to force God's hand: "Okay God, I get it, what you're teaching me is that you're going to disappoint me. Enough of this - just give me what I want!"

Maybe Adam could have resorted to Greed. He could have given up on God, walked away, and tried to find the answer to his loneliness himself. But there was nothing in all of creation that could fill the void of Eve's absence, and Adam is incapable of creating Eve. So if Adam had turned away from God, the results would have been catastrophic. Adam would have truly been completely alone, avoiding God because he thinks him to be cruel.

Finally, through Apathy, Adam could have simply called it quits. I imagine Adam sitting down on the dirt, grumpily refusing to name any more animals. Perhaps he would have told God that he preferred to be alone anyway, a sad attempt at denying the truth of his desire. This would have happened if Adam thought his desires were only there to make him suffer.

Consider the whole story from God's perspective. You know that if Adam sticks it out, he will be more delighted than he knew to be possible. But in the meantime, while he's struggling, what is this being you created doing? Is he showing you that he trusts you, is he giving up, trying to control you, or ditching you to do it himself? I think the stakes in this story are higher than we imagined. Adam's character, his relationship with God, is being proven. The only reason I believe we don't give this story more credit is because we know there's more to the story - the Fall. But here, in this moment, Adam's Faith shines. Adam turned towards God, continuing to have Faith in him, even after he had run out of possible candidates. To me, this story is a triumph of Faith.

This is a great example of desire handled with Faith. Adam felt the ache for a partner and trusted God to come through, despite coming up empty in the very task given to him by God. God honors Adam's perseverance in the very next verse by introducing him to Eve. He finally gets the fulfillment he was longing for, granted to him by God rather than by his own searching. This is the kind of Faith that God had in mind when he created us. We were made to be intelligent creatures capable of choosing how we handle our suffering, desires, and disappointments; and Faith is the best choice we have. But above all else God invites us to Faith because of his goodness, so that we learn to trust God in seasons when it's easy *and* when it seems impossible.

Enduring in Faith means that we linger in our sufferings, aching for fulfillment as we develop trust and perseverance, and finding hope in God. This matures us. Unlike children who cannot bear disappointment or suffering, we learn Faith through knowledge of God's dependability despite our circumstances. We develop character while we wait patiently for God to meet our needs as opposed to resorting to desperate measures, just as Adam demonstrated in his quest for Eve.

Understand, then, that some of the most damaging traumas happen to us when we are trusting and hopeful, only to find that the forces beyond our control conspired for our demise, not for our benefit. If the Enemy can convince us that Faith is foolhardy, then he has won a major victory. We cannot extend our arms outward in Faith while we are simultaneously covering where we've been wounded.

Because Faith is our natural state, it comes easily to us when we are whole. When we're young, innocent, and secure, we are (typically) predisposed to be both trusting of others and assertive with our desires. While hardship, betrayal, and evil can rob us of this security, healing can make Faith possible once more. This new, refined Faith, is more stable than the former, less experienced Faith. It is the same Faith that Peter holds in high esteem:

"...now for a little while you may have had to suffer grief in all kinds of trials. These have come so that the proven genuineness of your faith — of greater worth than gold, which perishes even though refined by fire — may result in praise, glory and honor..."

- 1 Peter 1:6-7 NIV

We are in dire need of healing from our grief and trials. We need God to heal us, and he promises to do so when we come to him. It isn't our job to heal ourselves. We cannot accomplish it through some sheer force of will. Healing requires our participation and acceptance, *not* that we have it all figured out. I would like to share with you some thoughts about what that healing is like, but first I must admit - healing looks different for everyone and every wound. Just when I think I've gotten the hang of how God heals my wounds, and I try to employ the same strategy over again, I find that healing through my own efforts escapes me. Healing is an interpersonal walk with God. And thank goodness. If it were anything else, if it were a rote check-up, no more organic than changing your car's oil, it would be insufficient to heal your unique human heart. That being said, there are some recognizable themes of healing that help us to discern when healing is available to us.

Recalling that Faith is central to our human nature, we can say that we all want to be seen for who we really are (vulnerable), and to be loved and accepted (secure). When we experience eye-opening trauma, these two forces are torn apart and come to be at odds with one another. Please note that the following paragraphs may be difficult or triggering for some individuals.

Let's use an example. Imagine that you are living in your home, in a neighborhood with people that you believe care about you. Your windows are open, you let the kids play out in the yard and with neighbors, and you don't sweat it if you forget to lock your door or close your garage. You feel connected and secure at all once. This state represents innocent Faith - like Adam and Eve in the Garden before the Fall, or like we are when we are young. But then your house gets broken into. You come home to find your personal space, and your feeling of safety and openness, violated. Prized possessions are stolen, many of your belongings lie shattered on the ground. Your heart gets torn in two.

Without healing, you go into a frenzy. The part of you that desires security kicks into overdrive. You buy new locks, install a home security system, buy a guard dog, put a fence with a gate around your home, shutter your windows, and sequester yourself inside your fortress. Paranoia and hyper-vigilance seeps in, and you start to wonder if maybe you've forgotten to secure something. You find yourself constantly checking to see if you're safe, tossing and turning late into the night as phantom imaginings of your home being broken into plague your mind. There's always more work to be done. This part of you vows never to be hurt again.

All the while, the vulnerable side of you withers. This part of you holds the pain of betrayal you felt. How could one of your neighbors do this to you? What did you do to deserve such horrible treatment? You long to be as innocent and naive as you once were, thereby being more connected with the people you've now cut off. This part of you wants to rest, longs to let your guard down, hopes beyond hope that someone can break down all the defenses that you've erected. This part longs to be held and told that everything will be okay.

As you can see, these two parts are divided against each other. The protective part demands security, and works to snuff out any hint of vulnerability for fear of getting hurt. The vulnerable part wants things to go back to the way things were, and despises the exhaustion inherent to being over-protective. The problem is that they are each partly right. Vulnerability knows that no amount of self-protection will ever be enough to completely guarantee safety. Protectiveness knows that to do nothing will only invite further harm.

Healing will elude us for as long as we ping-pong back and forth between the parts of our broken heart. Vulnerability will trigger the protective part to be anxious. Over-protection triggers the vulnerable part to be depressed. We wind up feeling trapped and hopeless. The goal of healing is not to be rid of either part, but rather to be whole. The divide between the parts, and the trauma that created the chasm, must be acknowledged and dealt with.

This is never something that God pushes us into. He will knock on doors that we might prefer him to ignore. But, God always honors our decision of whether or not we open the door to him. This decision, in and of itself, contributes towards our healing. And when the time is right, we learn to recognize and accept the broken parts of ourselves. Where we've come to despise the broken parts, God picks up the pieces and holds them near to his heart. He blesses our pain and draws near in a way that both exposes and honors us. He is the perfect remedy to our ambivalence and mistrust of others, at once both the right degree of bold, but also kind. He doesn't kick down our walls, he asks us to share with him what stories our walls tell.

And somewhere in the midst of the beautiful, messy process, we find that we have found more balance and freedom. The pain of the original wound feels more like a scar and less like an infection. We operate out of strengthened Faith - risking once more because our foundation of security and intimacy has shifted from a mirage to the solid rock.

If this has resonated with you, a helpful prayer might be: "God, my heart is broken. I'm tired of living in between my fear and my longings. I feel stuck. Would you come and help me? Be gentle with me, because my heart is tender. But I trust the pieces to you, God. Reveal to me the wounds I've carried, and all the ways I've tried to find healing on my own. I give you permission to work with me and within me. In Jesus' name, Amen."

How Faith Operates

Now that we've established that Faith is our natural and desired state of being and that when we've lived enough life, healing is required for Faith, we are ready to discuss how to choose to live in Faith. If we return to the Forging Character Quadrants, we see that Faith is the product of the choice to take personal action combined with inviting others to participate in our search for fulfillment. Hence, Faith exists in the intersection between a sense of vulnerability (allowing others to see us), and confidence (boldly advocating for oneself). Because matured Faith, which has undergone healing, knows the risks inherent to Faith, we come ready to deal with disappointment. This open-eyed Faith allows us to be honest and for others to act freely.

For example, consider inviting a friend over to watch a movie you're excited about. If they say no, the two different responses are to either continue in Faith, or to self protect:

"That's okay, is there something else you'd like to do together?" Faith might also say: "I feel pretty disappointed that you don't want to watch a movie with me. Can we talk some more about this?"

Or, we can self protect in all its various forms:

"Fine! Forget I even asked, I'll just watch it by myself. Who needs you anyway?!"

"That's okay, I didn't really want to watch a movie."

"I did what you wanted to last time, so now you owe watching a movie with me."

The former response shows that the ultimate desire the person has is for friendship and honesty. The activity of watching a movie together isn't the priority, maintaining the integrity of the relationship is. Faith does not confuse, "I don't want to watch a movie," for, "I don't care about you." The latter responses show the exact opposite attitude - that the rejected party has internalized the declined invitation and is sabotaging the friendship because they didn't get what they wanted. When the other person operates in their free will, with their own opinions and desires, they assign blame: that either that the other person is out of line, or that they were foolish for asking in the first place.

This blame-shifting is commonplace in the midst of disappointment. We almost automatically try to find something to justify our pain, whether we take the blame or lay it at others' feet. Neither is helpful. It is only bargaining - a point in our grief journey showing that we haven't yet reached a point of closure. In order to move past the criticism, anger, and disgust we externalize or internalize, we must more objectively evaluate our discontent and excavate down to the core issues.

As such, Faith is the only quadrant that prioritizes healthy relationships over the gratification of desire. In other words, Faith would prefer to be hurt rather than either not risking being hurt or controlling what others do. Why on Earth would we choose this? Manipulation and Greed prioritize personal fulfillment over relational quality; Apathy cultivates neither fulfillment nor relational growth, but sabotages each in an attempt to minimize pain. But Faith invites disappointment in order to find fulfillment. There are two reasons for this.

First, Faith puts more stock in quality relationships than in the fulfillment of personal desire. In other words, a genuine relationship because the overriding desire. Consider if you were inviting someone to go to your favorite restaurant. While you certainly desire the food, the thing you care about more, in Faith, is the relationship. If the person you're inviting would prefer to not go and do something else instead, you're more likely to be flexible. You're ready to take on the "disappointment" of not going to your favorite restaurant because you'd rather be together. Obviously there's tremendous risk involved in this style of interaction. Faith trusts, but it is not the same thing as allowing yourself to be taken advantage of. Without trust, it would be impossible.

Second, Faith understands that even if you were to push for your desires to be met (by accessing one of the other Quadrants), it wouldn't be the same. *Force* the other person to come to the restaurant with you, and your evening will be ruined. Forget inviting others altogether, and your loneliness will rob you of joy. Faith, as out of our control as it is, is our best shot at finding fulfillment. It is a kind, persistent advocacy of our desires, met with a readiness to lie our desires down for the sake of peace.

To operate in Faith I must find a way to take responsibility for my desire while also recognizing others' free will as I involve them in my search for fulfillment. Let's say that I find myself thirsty and wanting a glass of water. I can take responsibility for my desire when I interact with someone by merely stating what my desire is: "Hello! I'd like a glass of water." By communicating what I want, I allow myself to be known. This can be a risky thing at times. It may not feel too vulnerable to be open about the desire for a glass of water, but consider how it might feel to tell someone that you're interested in them romantically! It's a big gamble to let other people know of your desires.

Faith is willing to be known, which means having the openness to communicate desires that are important to us even if those desires seem outlandish or unrealistic. In being forthright with desire, Faith is similar to Greed in that it requires us to take personal action steps to work towards the fulfillment of our desires. Unlike Greed, however, Faith chooses to involve others in finding fulfillment.

Let's continue with the example. Now that I've named my desire by saying "I'd like a glass of water," I let the other person know that I'd like their help by making a request: "Would you mind getting me one?" By involving others in our search for fulfillment, Faith bears a resemblance to Manipulation. But Faith differs from Manipulation because Faith respects others' free will rather than seeking to control them. In fact, Faith anticipates that others will operate based on their free will, and accounts for it in how we make requests. To show that my request is genuine, and not manipulative, I may add: "And it's okay with me if you'd rather not."

Faith, at its core, is a vulnerable request. It is freely open to any outcome. Although the preferred outcome may be obvious, the requests that Faith makes doesn't put pressure on others' choices. God desires for us to come to him with such requests. Jesus teaches us:

"Ask and it will be given to you; seek and you will find; knock and the door will be opened to you. For everyone who asks receives; the one who seeks finds; and to the one who knocks, the door will be opened.

"Which of you, if your son asks for bread, will give him a stone? Or if he asks for a fish, will give him a snake? If you, then, though you are evil, know how to give good gifts to your children, how much more will your Father in heaven give good gifts to those who ask him!"

- Matthew 7:7-11 NIV

Jesus wants us to ask our Father, in Faith, for the things we desire. These requests are based in the belief of God's goodness, and don't demand that God prove his goodness to us by granting our requests as we see fit. True Faith prefers that others' actions are based upon their honest choice, not based on compulsion or pressure. We do not put God to the test - which would really just be Manipulation.

Our Faith itself must also be genuine and honest. If the person I'm asking were to say to me, "Not right now, but thanks for asking," and I got upset with them, I show that my Faith was deceitful - that it truly wasn't okay with me if they denied my request, and that I only acted as though it was. Faith seems counterintuitive as a means of gratifying desire because it openly acknowledges that others may reject our requests. But it does so because if others take the action that we requested of them, we can definitively know that they have done so of their own volition. The knowledge that others have done as we have asked, specifically because they freely chose to do so, makes all the difference to the fulfillment we feel. When the person I'm asking for a glass of water says, "Sure, here you go!" and hands me a glass of water, I can be sure of three things that lead me to experience genuine fulfillment.

First, I will feel a sense of positive self-esteem. This comes from having opened myself up by expressing my desire, and it ending well. Remember, it is always a risk when we let others know what we are feeling, desiring, and hoping for. In this case, the gamble paid off. It feels tremendously good when you take a risk in being honest and that honesty is honored. I can now breathe a sigh of relief. Again, this relief is minor when we consider the request a glass of water, but imagine how you might feel with a more vulnerable or revealing desire. For example, if I told someone that

I wanted to go skydiving with them, and they chastise my desire as mere adrenaline-junkie foolishness, I might feel a sting of embarrassment. I might then work to conceal my desire from them. On the other hand, being responded to with warmth and openness encourages us to be more open. Communicating honest desire is a risk, and it doesn't always go the way we want it to. When it does, however, the choice to have Faith feels rewarding.

If the first component of our fulfillment comes from the fruition of our personal actions, then the second component comes from others' actions. When I receive my glass of water through Faith, I know that the person gave me what I wanted because they chose to do so, not because they were forced or coerced into doing so. This means that their actions demonstrate something remarkable - that the person truly cares. Having heard my desire, and knowing that they could turn away, they chose to turn towards the request. For human beings created to exist in meaningful and healthy relationships, this is a big deal! Coupled with the first level of fulfillment, this second factor makes for a meaningful, trusting relationship that helps us continue the difficult feat of living in Faith.

The third factor I experience when I find fulfillment through Faith is the simple gratification of my desire. Since Faith prioritizes healthy relationships, I get a double helping of contentment from the desire for quality relating and the desire that led to the interaction in the first place - my thirst. I feel happy about how I got to the glass of water. I gratefully drink it, and feel satisfaction as my thirst is quenched.

Following the first two layers of fulfillment, found from being open about my desires and knowing that someone else cares, this third layer is the icing on the cake. Icing is sweet, but it doesn't fill us up. For that, we need to feel positively about ourselves and our relationships. Gratifying our base desires keeps us alive, but never makes our lives meaningful. Meaning cannot be found in having limitless water, but only in being true to who we are and by nurturing loving relationships. Here is what this all reveals: true fulfillment is obtained by *how* we reach our goals, not by *whether* we reach them. The means we use makes the difference between a success that can be enjoyed, or a "success" that also brings either overriding anxiety or guilt. Faith can truly enjoy the gratification of desire because the path it took to that success was bold, kind, and honorable.

But Faith can also operate when we experience disappointment, when we are told no. Faith responds to adversity by bolstering us, spurring us to remain hopeful. Conversely, disappointment, especially when it is recurrent, can become our excuse in allowing our Faith to crumble away. When our desires are unmet, we face a choice: we can continue to operate in Faith, or we can change the means of how we're behaving under the guise of "self protection."

Self protection is a defensive reaction to disappointment by vowing to ourselves that we will not be hurt again. Self protection tells us that Faith only opens us to the possibility of pain, and that we are "better off playing it safe." However, self protection doesn't help us to find fulfillment, it only moves us into one of the other three quadrants. In fact, fulfillment is completely sacrificed the moment we give up on Faith because no other means of seeking fulfillment takes the proper route. They may seem "safe" in comparison to Faith, but they lead nowhere. The means spoil the end.

Maintaining Faith despite disappointment does not mean that we continue to open ourselves to someone who harms us. To have Faith, we must have the option of walking away and drawing boundaries for our benefit, and the benefit of others. Without this power, the relationship is abusive - not based on Faith. Faith can self-advocate, and even limit interactions with particular things or people. But it doesn't go as far as caccooning self-protection, which treats relationships and desires with broad strokes of suspicion. For example: When disappointed, Faith may cause us to ask someone else the same question, but self-protection causes us to label others as entirely undependable.

The most drastic form of self protection is Apathy, which exchanges the possibility of fulfillment for the guarantee of disappointment. Apathy assumes that control (even if it only leads to disappointment) is better than the risk of having your hopes thwarted. But the risk of disappointment also comes with a chance for fulfillment. Apathy gives up on that chance. When something good happens you can control whether or not you enjoy it, which is exactly what Apathy does - for the detriment of those who use it. They choose not to enjoy the goodness around them because they cannot control it.

Manipulation and Greed are used for self protection by assuming that other people are unreliable, and so they must either be controlled or avoided to find fulfillment. Control and avoidance, however, fail to bring us the goodness we desire. When we try to dictate what others do, it only leaves us bitter. When we avoid others, using self-gratification to meet our needs, it leaves us hollow.

But Faith that endures disappointment testifies that fulfillment is bigger than the sole gratification of desire. Increasing Faith continues to hope and trust despite the current circumstances. It is able to take protective measures without altering course so significantly that fulfillment becomes impossible. Ultimately, responding to disappointment with Faith shows that our hope is not in the present circumstances, but in God.

For example, consider inviting a friend over to watch a movie you're excited about. If they say no, the two different responses are to either continue in Faith, or to self protect:

"That's okay, is there something else you'd like to do together?" Faith might also say: "I feel pretty disappointed that you don't want to watch a movie with me. Can we talk some more about this?"

Or, we can self protect in all its various forms:

"Fine! Forget I even asked, I'll just watch it by myself. Who needs you anyway?!"
"That's okay, I didn't really want to watch a movie."
"I did what you wanted to last time, so now you owe watching a movie with me."

The former response shows that the ultimate desire the person has is for friendship and honesty. The activity of watching a movie together isn't the priority, maintaining the integrity of the relationship is. The latter responses show the exact opposite attitude - that the rejected party has internalized the declined invitation and is sabotaging the friendship because they didn't get what they wanted. Faith does not confuse, "I don't want to watch a movie," for, "I don't care about you." When the other person operates in their free will, with their own opinions and desires, they assign blame: that either that the other person is out of line, or that they were foolish for asking in the first place.

This blame-shifting is commonplace in the midst of disappointment. We almost automatically try to find something to justify our pain, whether we take the blame or lay it at others' feet. Neither is helpful. It is only bargaining - a point in our grief journey showing that we haven't yet reached a point of closure. In order to move past the criticism, anger, and disgust we externalize or internalize, we must excavate down to the core issues of what it means to have Faith.

Increasing Faith

Faith means being able to trust God even when we are disappointed. Although we might not be happy about our disappointment, maintaining Faith in him shows that we still believe in God's goodness. This can be incredibly difficult, especially when the situation seems dire or neverending, and God feels far away. And yet, this is the main theme of the Bible, and the principle hope that Christians have: that when all seems lost, God comes through. It is our Faith that death, which according to all scientific study appears to be the final, morbid conclusion to our existence, is not the end.

Christian Faith is different from worldly Faith. We believe that disappointment is not the last word. That, according to God's promises, the goodness we desire will not be met with "no," but instead "not yet." As such, Christians' ability to endure disappointment shows that we are looking ahead with confidence, maintaining that even if we die, God will meet our desires perfectly. Maintaining Faith supposes that disappointment is only the prelude to eventual fulfillment. How we manage our disappointments, then, is really all about how we handle our desires.

It is uncomfortable to want something in the first place - to have a desire. The discomfort of feeling desire is nearly identical to the feeling of when we discover we are unable to have what we want. Disappointment only means that we will continue to live with the desires we had in the first place. So, if we do not trust God when we are disappointed, then we also won't trust God with our desires in general. Disappointment only makes our disposition more pronounced.

Handling desire by trusting God despite our setbacks redefines how we view our trials. Our deepest desires shift from self-seeking gratification, to the development of maturity by maintaining a quality relationship with God even when life is difficult. In other words, in our immaturity we are only concerned with ending our trials as quickly as possible. But when we mature, we learn to be patient in our trials and seek closeness with God as opposed to the easiest way out. In our sin and selfishness, we imagine that our desires are there only for our own pleasures. But as we grow in our relationship to God and truly come to understand his goodness, we become more concerned with loving God. Subsequently, as we delight ourselves in God regardless of our fulfillment or disappointment, we find that God is able to satisfy us either way.

Adam's test of faith developed his perseverance, and his patience ultimately led to his fulfillment in God. The Bible asserts that the same is true for us - that our trials can lead to growth and maturity as we learn to have Faith:

Consider it pure joy, my brothers and sisters, whenever you face trials of many kinds, because you know that the testing of your faith produces perseverance. Let perseverance finish its work so that you may be mature and complete, not lacking anything.

- James 1:2-4 NIV

James' assertion is that if we allow perseverance to "finish its work," if we stay faithful to God in the midst of trials, that we will lack nothing. Perseverance itself doesn't grant us completion, but creates space for God to work in our hearts as we become more sure of our security in him rather than in ourselves. This sounds noble in theory, but in reality perseverance is incredibly difficult. During trials we often think that something has gone wrong when the turmoil isn't letting up. It's easy to make negative assumptions like: "God must not care about me," or "I must not be praying hard enough." The assumption that trials are bad limits us because we focus on our pain and not our growth. We forget that God is after more than our mere comfort. He desires for us to be mature, able to look beyond our own comfort or discomfort.

God tested Adam's faith by challenging him to endure in his hope for a suitable helper while naming the creatures. When Adam demonstrated his faith by enduring disappointment after disappointment, God gave him the perfect solution to his desire: Eve (To be clear, Eve has *far* greater value and purpose than merely satiating Adam's loneliness.). Like Adam looking for a suitable helper, God wants us to trust him with our desires even when fulfillment escapes us. That trust shows that our hearts worship God not solely because of our comfort, but out of a conviction that God is good whether we are comfortable or not. When God allows your life to be comfortable it is easy to love God. But when life is difficult, when we find ourselves in situations we didn't want or ask for, our capacity to love God testifies to what we truly believe about God. The principle of accusing God when times are rough is the very thing that Satan tries to use to his advantage:

> *Then the LORD said to Satan, "Have you considered my servant Job? There is no one on Earth like him; he is blameless and upright, a man who fears God and shuns evil."*
>
> *"Does Job fear God for nothing?" Satan replied. "Have you not put a hedge around him and his household and everything he has? You have blessed the work of his hands, so that his flocks and herds are spread throughout the land. But stretch out your hand and strike everything he has, and he will surely curse you to your face."*
>
> *- Job 1:8-11 NIV*

Translation: Satan claims that Job worships God only because his life is easy. If his life were bitter, Satan claims that Job will lose his faith and turn against God. In other words, Satan accuses mankind of loving God so long as it is convenient to them. So God permits Satan to test Job. Later on, when Job's livelihood lies in tatters all around him, this is how Job responds:

> *"Shall we accept good from God, and not trouble?"*
>
> *- Job 2:10 NIV*

Job submits to God, and makes clear his conviction that God is good even if his present circumstances seem to say otherwise. When we increase our Faith, we choose to continue trusting God by patiently waiting for him to bring fulfillment even though waiting may be agonizing. No one trusts someone that is out to harm them. Thus, enduring in Faith means that we testify our belief in God's goodness. This is hard to do when we find ourselves presented with evidence that seems contrary - that God is *not* good. The only way we can have enduring Faith is to have deeply known, felt, and experienced the love of God.

Another crucial factor in our response to disappointment is the recognition that true fulfillment can only be found in God. In other words, it's understanding that turning away from God isn't any more likely to help us find fulfillment. Increasing Faith comes with the knowledge that any gratification found outside of Faith (and a positive relationship with God), does not satisfy, such as if Adam had attempted to make Eve himself. A lump of clay shaped like a woman doesn't compare to the woman God fashioned himself! Similarly, our choice when we are disappointed is to either continue aching for true fulfillment or attempt to satiate our longings with man-made alternatives. Where the former is defined by Faith, the latter is characterized by Manipulation and Greed. The choice between longsuffering endurance and lustful alternatives creates tension which can make it seem as though God is tempting us. However, James 1:13-14 NIV says:

"When tempted, no one should say, 'God is tempting me.' For God cannot be tempted by evil, nor does he tempt anyone; but each one is tempted when, by his own evil desire, he is dragged away and enticed."

James affirms that God is not the source of temptation. Temptation occurs when we are drawn away from God and instead seek gratification even if it means disobeying God. This occurs when we become convinced that we can find gratification away from God. We must be cautious when we consider what is meant by "evil desires" in this verse. I contend that desires are determined to be either good or evil on the basis of whether they submit to God's authority, not whether they feel either good or bad. Consider that Peter was rebuked by Jesus for saying "no" to Jesus' proclamation of his own suffering, death, and resurrection. Peter likely thought he was being empathetic, but his desire was out of sync with God's will. Desires aren't evil because they have a bad nature, but because they don't stay faithful to God.

James continues by explaining what happens when our desires stray from God:

"Then, after desire has conceived, it gives birth to sin; and sin, when it is full-grown, gives birth to death."

- James 1:15 NIV

Sin occurs when we turn to alternative forms of gratification by using Manipulation, Greed, or Apathy rather than having Faith by trusting God. The effort to find fulfillment outside of the will of God always ends in vain. Sin sets us on a hamster wheel of disappointment - constantly running after gratification of our desires, but never finding anything substantial. It is little surprise that the end result of sin is death. Manipulation and Greed lose the ability to love God and trust him, but they actually do maintain the capacity for hope. That hope is not placed in God, however, but in sin. Hoping that sin will gratify your desires is a game you can't win; sin will *always* leave you disappointed. We are created to find our desires met in the living God, the Wellspring of Life. When we try to treat them on our own we are left trying to douse a raging fire with a garden hose.

If we are looking for wellness in the midst of a life filled with desire, then we cannot afford to abandon God. If we do so, continual disappointment coupled with a refusal to trust God eventually leads us into Apathy, where we finally lose hope. It would seemingly be easier if we didn't have any choice *but* to trust God. However, God allows us to choose where we look for fulfillment. He alone holds the key to our fulfillment, but he doesn't demand that we come to him. Neither does God tempt us to give into the sinful, "easy answers." He gives us free will to either turn towards him or away from him.

God doesn't have the same agenda that the world has. He is not out for efficiency, comfort, or instant gratification. Rather, he's interested in the maturation of our character and the quality of our relationship with him. Disappointment, tragedy, and evil can cause us to doubt God's goodness, and our doubt tempts us to take matters into our own hands. These things create a stark fork in the road where we can continue to trust God despite our uncertainty, or we can try to take matters into our own hands.

Clinging to God through Faith, despite setbacks and doubt, is *the* most difficult task in our lives. It is a choice that flies in the face of our every instinct, which urge us to self-protect. The Bible, however, calls us to endure. Though not by putting up walls - we endure by maintaining hope and Faith. Faith is the only way that we can endure hardships and still find meaning. God created mankind to be able to choose to have Faith in him, but we need help and healing. So far we've been using Adam as an example of how to respond to adversity with Faith, but everyone knows he isn't exactly the perfect model of Faith. We need someone that we can relate to and be inspired by. We need a power that can move within us, compelling us to Faith and love, born of an undying hope. We need Jesus.

The Author and Perfecter of Faith

What do you suppose is the ultimate example of Faith in the Bible? Most of the people I ask the question to give the answer of Jesus' crucifixion - and for good reason. Jesus' choice to endure suffering and death for our salvation is miraculous - and even that is an understatement! Words fail to describe the cross. It is at once both breathtaking and terrible.

Yet, I find Jesus' prayer in the Garden of Gethsemane to be, for me, the climactic moment of Faith. At the last supper, Jesus had prophesied about his betrayal, death, and resurrection. He knows what's coming. After the meal, he takes Peter, James, and John with him to the Mount of Olives to pray:

Then he said to them, "My soul is overwhelmed with sorrow to the point of death. Stay here and keep watch with me." Going a little farther, he fell with his face to the ground and prayed, "My Father, if it is possible, may this cup be taken from me. Yet not as I will, but as you will."

- Matthew 26:38-39 NIV

So what exactly is Jesus requesting? Isaiah 51:22 NIV sheds light on what Jesus means by taking away "this cup":

This is what your Sovereign LORD says, your God, who defends his people: "See, I have taken out of your hand the cup that made you stagger; from that cup, the goblet of my wrath, you will never drink again."

It's obvious that Jesus is not asking for a physical cup to be removed from his person. He is asking to be excused from the crucifixion, where he will become the object of God's fury towards sin. Remember that he shortly ago rebuked Peter for suggesting something similar. Yet here he is, asking and surrendering:

A second time He went away and prayed, "My Father, if this cannot pass unless I drink it, may Your will be done."
- Matthew 26:42 ESV

Jesus knows that all things are possible for God. So he asks that, if it is somehow possible, that he might not have to take up the entirety of human sin and die upon the cross. Even still, Jesus acknowledges that he will be obedient to God even if his request cannot be granted.

What's remarkable to me is that this prayer is similar to Peter's words in Matthew 16:22, where he rebukes Jesus for predicting the crucifixion, and tells him that it will never happen. Jesus' response, "Get behind me, Satan! You are a stumbling block to me; you do not have in mind the concerns of God, but merely human concerns." (Matt. 16:23), was surely a stinging reprimand. Peter's assertion that Jesus "never" be put to death is similar to Jesus' request to have the cup pass from him. Yet one sentiment is satanic, and the other is divine.

Just my two cents here, but I believe this had everything to do with the posture they each had. Peter sought to take control of Jesus' destiny, whereas Jesus laid down his request before the Father. I believe we find ourselves facing similar challenges. Will we demand gratification of our needs and desires, or are we willing to have Faith? It is not so much what we want that matters, but how we manage what we want. Demanding things happen exactly as we desire is godless, selfish, and immature. Conversely, no matter how audacious the request, God welcomes us to be honest about our desires so long as we also submit ourselves to God's will.

Regardless of how properly Jesus' frames his request, God's answer was still "no." Yet Jesus maintains his Faith in God not only knowing that his request was denied, but also that it would mean his torment and death. The only way to make sense of such radical Faith is to understand that Jesus trusted that his Father was good and had a plan - even if the outcome looked bleak from his own perspective.

Romans 8:9 explains that, as Christians, we have the Spirit of Christ living in us. Whenever we operate in Faith, the Spirit causes us to act akin to the Faith of Christ: willing us to be both honest and obedient to God. But in reality, how honest and how obedient are we willing to be? Personally, I find Jesus' prayer in the Garden to be both extraordinarily comforting and absolutely terrifying at the same time. It is incredibly exposing to be totally transparent with desire and alarming to truly let go of control. Yet the notion of complete transparency and trust stirs something within me that knows this is how life is meant to be. Why is something that seems so natural also so contrary to the way we act?

All too often we're not really honest with God about what we truly want. We strive to find ways to make deals with God or use dishonesty to cover up the desires we assume God disapproves of. Yet every desire within us, when operating in the way that God intended, points us Heavenwards. We do not examine our desires deeply enough to realize this fact. Instead, we work to manipulate God or others for our own gratification. We think that if we can just state our request the right way, with enough justification or righteousness, maybe we can convince God to do what we want. This strikes me as a far departure from praying as though your Father already intimately knows what you want:

"And when you pray, do not keep on babbling like pagans, for they think they will be heard because of their many words. Do not be like them, for your Father knows what you need before you ask him."
- Matthew 6:7-8 NIV

Deep down we desire all kinds of things, but we chastise ourselves for thinking of making those requests known to God if we believe they are outside of his will. So we keep those desires quiet, buried deep down. Thus we distance ourselves from God. The beliefs that God doesn't really care and that we aren't good enough for God begin to creep in. We need a way out of this trap - neither remaining silent nor attempting manipulating God for our own gratification. Luckily, Jesus demonstrates how to handle desire faithfully - he is completely honest with God about his radical desire, yet submits to God's authority.

If there is any request contrary to the will of God, then it has to be the notion that Jesus would not have died on the cross. The death, resurrection, and ascension of Jesus are *pivotal* to God's work with all of mankind - and Jesus asks to opt out! Without these things, there would be no saving grace, no reconciliation with God, no salvation, no adoption as sons and daughters of God. We would still be left in our sin and separated from God. I propose that there could be no greater thing which would be contrary to the will of God than Jesus' request. Nothing we could possibly ask for could close to the sheer audacity of it. And yet if Jesus is so bold as to ask God that "this cup" be taken from him, then why are we so hesitant with asking God for requests that, by comparison, are markedly insignificant?

In fact, Paul admonishes:

"Do not be anxious about anything, but in every situation, by prayer and petition, with thanksgiving, present your requests to God."
- Philippians 4:6 NIV

It bears restating: In *every* situation make your requests known to God. But it is not enough to merely state our requests to God. We must also be willing to trust God and be obedient to him:

Trust in the LORD with all your heart and lean not on your own understanding...
- Proverbs 3:5a NIV

Jesus was honest with God about a desire he knew was contrary to God's will, and was also obedient to God even when it meant his death. If that's not Faith, I don't know what is. When we have done everything that we can to communicate our preferences to God, all that's left to do is trust him by accepting whatever outcome he deems fit. We make a choice to endure in Faith by trusting God in full awareness that things may not go the way we want them to. Faith accepts the risk of trusting God. These are the moments when we let go of the rock wall, run out of animals to name, plead with God in the middle of the night, and echo the words of Christ:

"Shall I not drink the cup the Father has given me?"
- John 18:11b NIV

Setting our eyes on Christ and his example of Faith, we become more intentional about submitting our desires while also developing resiliency to endure suffering. This maturity occurs as we choose to trust God by being honest with him about our deepest dreams and submitting our compulsion to control the outcome. It's about a real, authentic relationship with God - one in which going through the motions won't cut it. As we become more in tune with our heart's longings and learn to communicate our requests, our relationship with God grows. This changes suffering into an exercise of trust. Affliction becomes the crucible where we cling to God, forging our character in the same mold as the one who perfected intimacy with God despite immense suffering: Jesus Christ.

If there were any doubt to God's goodness, Jesus tips the scale. As many theologians have observed, because of Jesus' Faith and suffering we can definitively say that God can empathize with us. In other words, if God were only ever perfect and never experienced suffering, it would be difficult to accept that God wants us to trust him while we ourselves are suffering. Faith, which is able to endure suffering while maintaining obedience to God, is only possible when we truly believe that God is good. So, when the outcome isn't what we wanted or asked for, we may begin to doubt his goodness and pull away from him. We start to protect ourselves from our desires and from God. The draw to self protect lures us away from God and from true selves, robbing us of any kind of meaningful fulfillment.

Life constantly throws situations at us that require us to choose whether or not we will live in Faith. It is not as though once we learn to live in Faith that our lives suddenly become any easier. Choosing Faith will not convince God to make our problems go away. Faith is merely a choice to recognize God's goodness by placing trust in him. In fact, if we assume that choosing Faith means that our lives become easier, we will be sadly disappointed. Maintaining Faith means coming to terms with the negative outcomes we otherwise fear. Adam's dilemma did not suddenly stop when he trusted God in Faith. The point of Faith is not to make matters easier, but to enjoy intimacy with God. God does not use difficulty to punish us, nor does he remove it to reward us for "good behavior." After Satan's rebellion and the Fall, trouble has been interwoven into our reality. Manipulation and Greed futilely expend our energy as they frantically try to ensure a positive outcome despite the fact that a positive outcome cannot be gained through those means. But where Manipulation and Greed fight for control, Apathy lays down arms, assuming that defeat is inevitable. Faith is unique in that it maintains hope without demanding control. Choosing Faith allows trouble to refine who we are becoming. Faith is the most difficult stance to take towards life, and it is only possible through the healing and love of a God who is undoubtedly good.

Verse to remember: *"Do not be anxious about anything, but in every situation, by prayer and petition, with thanksgiving, present your requests to God." Philippians 4:6 NIV*

Thought to consider: Faith vulnerably expresses desire while submitting to others' free will. When fulfilled through faith, the pleasure is genuine. When disappointed, Faith is unique in that it maintains hope without demanding control. Disappointment can lead us to self protect, which moves us into other quadrants.

Questions to ponder:

- Which of your hopes or desires have you been hesitant to take before God?
- How can we manage the immense risk that we take by letting go of control?
- Where has disappointment caused you to lose hope?

Chapter 3

MANIPULATION

The getting of treasures by a lying tongue is a fleeting vapor and a snare of death. The violence of the wicked will sweep them away, because they refuse to do what is just.

- Proverbs 21:6-7 ESV

My dear brothers and sisters, take note of this: Everyone should be quick to listen, slow to speak and slow to become angry, because human anger does not produce the righteousness that God desires.

- James 1:19-20 NIV

The Culture of Manipulation

A quote from *Richard Evans' quote book*[1] reads:

"People may forget what you say.
They may forget what you did,
but people will never forget
how you made them feel."

- Carl Buehner

Well, I remember three things from my 7th grade Tech class: building and programming a small robot, watching the live events of 9/11 (our classroom had one of the few TVs in the school), and the day I sent my teacher into a fit of rage.

And boy do I remember how I felt the day I ticked off my Tech teacher.

I had a couple of friends in my Tech class, and one day we were doing work in a small computer room connected to the larger tech classroom where our teacher was. As middle schoolers will do under little supervision, we were goofing off within minutes - spinning and racing in our computer chairs all over the room. For whatever reason, we thought it would be funny to zoom in and out of the room on our computer chairs and slam the door on each other, locking one of us out at a time. To be fair, we *were* creating quite a ruckus. That was when our teacher descended upon us. He was a mustached, girthy fellow, and was terrifying to my scrawny, 7th-grade self Seeing his face turn an impressive shade of red and contorted with barely constrained rage was enough to turn our fun into dread. My face probably turned white to complement his red.

I don't recall any chiding one might expect: "Hey guys, knock it out. Focus on your work," only a zero-to-one-hundred kind of anger, as if I had just insulted his mother. I don't remember what he said. I don't remember if he yelled, or even if we were punished. I just remember his face and the terror that ran through my veins like ice. After that day, there wasn't any more goofing off in Tech. I was kept in line out of fear, which motivated me to do whatever it took to avoid another kind of incident like that in the future.

Whatever this interaction was - it was not based in Faith. For the record, I don't blame my teacher for not putting Faith in a bunch of hyperactive 7th graders. Fear is a healthy thing in moderation. It helps us to learn about the dangers in life, and it catalyzes our Fight or Flight Response when we need it during life-threatening situations. But this process can be hijacked and used against us, operating in ways that it was never meant to. Fear can become a way of life. Fear might keep a classroom in line, it even may stop some from breaking laws. But fear *oppresses*. It cannot give us abundant life. God does not intend for us to live in fear:

> *For God gave us a spirit not of fear but of power and love and self-control.*
> *-2 Timothy 1:7 ESV*

Fear makes us believe that life is dangerous, and so motivates us to do everything in our power to mitigate danger by exerting control or fleeing from danger. Hence the Fight or Flight Response. It is the desire for control that we'll be examining in this chapter. Manipulation is the "Fight" part of the Fight or Flight Response, and compels us to use anger, force, aggression, power, guilt, or coercion to control others.

Manipulation ultimately stems from fear, especially the fear of being out of control. We arrive in Manipulation as a result of a self-protecting belief which holds that others are needed, but not to be trusted. Manipulation keeps others at arm's length, exchanging real intimacy (which allows others the possibility to disappoint us) for the illusion of "safe predictability," seemingly attained through efforts to control.

We have all been both subject to Manipulation, and wielders of Manipulation. No human escapes it because it is simply part of our inherited sin-nature. This is no more apparent than in young children. As we develop communication skills we begin to form simple requests with one or two word sentences: "Have it?" or "Go outside?" These interactions begin as Faith - the very Faith that God hardwired us to have. But just watch what happens when you tell that child, "no." Things change in the blink of an eye. The child throws a tantrum, screaming and crying for what they want. They may try to take what they want anyway. They might fall to the floor, wailing and pounding their fists. They do not yet have the capacity to manage the disappointment and frustration about not getting their desires met, so kids throw a tantrum. Unfortunately, many adults do the same thing! How did humanity get here?

We have lost Eden, the place where things came easily. But now the world no longer conforms nicely to our whims. We may have hearts that were meant for Faith but we find ourselves in unfamiliar and unforgiving territory. Even people themselves have become dangerous and untrustworthy. So, instead of inviting others to change by communicating our requests flexibly, we try to *force* change in the world around us. Even at a young age, when Faith fails us, we resort to Manipulation.

Similarly to how fear can serve a functional purpose, there are plenty of moments where Manipulation may be entirely acceptable. For instance, I'm not going to ask someone if they would mind looking across the street if I see them about to run headfirst into traffic. I'm going to either yank them back or yell at them to stop! In the same way, there are lots of interactions with those in authority where we readily accept their Manipulation. Nobody waits for the police officer to ask nicely before pulling over. To an extent, this kind of Manipulation relies on a socially unspoken, but lawfully dictated agreement between the manipulator and those being manipulated. The manipulator bears responsibility to treat their power with care, and those being manipulated are expected to respect the authority of the manipulator.

Today's society is founded in Manipulation, and for good reason. Human beings, when given the choice between right and wrong, will inevitably choose to do wrong. If civilization as it currently exists were governed by Faith, the trust we place in one another would be abused. Human laws help us to be self-governing and live in a world where, ideally, the strong are not able to prey upon the weak. There is no asking nicely when it comes to obeying the law.

Manipulation may be as overt as mankind's laws, or so subtle as to be barely distinguishable from Faith. There are many faces of Manipulation, and we need to be able to call some of them out. We could never identify *all* the different ways people manipulate. But, at the very minimum, the pattern of Manipulation is to communicate desires as commands rather than requests. It is the subtle shift from: "Can we go outside?" to "Let's go outside." Requests imply we understand that others have free will, and may choose to tell us no. Commands, however, attempt to remove the possibility for others to deny us. Commands are not open to disagreement. The critical feature differentiating a demand from a request is the tone and context in which we communicate. You could make a veiled command by altering your tone of voice: "Do you *think* you could hand me a tissue?" Manipulation works most powerfully in our implied meaning. It forces the person being manipulated to envision, and therefore internalize, what would be incurred for insubordination. This oftentimes causes the party being manipulated to feel guilty for even contemplating disobedience.

Guilting is a passive-aggressive form of Manipulation that uses the emotions or obligations of another person to control them. Here's what it looks like: "If you *really* cared about me, you'd _____," or "It would just mean *so* much to me if you'd _____." Guilting plays off others' conscious, putting them into a position where, if they deny you, they are made to feel like the bad guy. Guilting makes others pay for rejecting your demands, where the person being manipulated is blamed for any trouble being caused. It is a crafty and subtle form of Manipulation that is very difficult to disarm, as the manipulator may defend their words as "an innocent request" or "honesty." They defend their actions as Faith without acknowledging the manipulative results being felt by the people around them.

A critical distinction between Manipulation and Faith is that Manipulation punishes whereas Faith protects. Protecting and punishing can look similar - the difference is that protecting is about fair action that we take ourselves, where punishment is controlling someone else. For instance, compare the same sentiment expressed in two different ways: "Don't you dare cheat on me again, or else we're through!" or "I won't be a part of an unfaithful relationship, though I am willing to give you one more chance." While the decision is the same (to leave the relationship if the partner cheats again), the former threatens and tries to control and punish, whereas the latter clarifies what the speaker is willing and not willing to do.

Manipulation is not only using commands, but also taking it to another level by employing anger, rage, violence, threats, punishment, or intimidation to subjugate others into doing their will: "You *will* do as I tell you, or else!" These demands generally are used by those who believe they have the authority to boss others around.

On the other hand, Manipulation may take on the appearance of pleading, begging, whining, or criticizing. These pestering tactics are used by people who try to wear down others into giving in to their demands. It is primarily used by people who feel that they do not have as much authority as those they are petitioning. This type of manipulator will counter your noncompliance with petulance until you've had enough and cave in, just to get them to stop bothering you. This strategy runs deep in our psychology - often to the point where we're not even aware that we're doing it.

The bottom line is that Manipulation abuses power, emotions, relationships, trust, and most importantly, people. It is a tactic used to remove free will from others, attempting to force people into doing what we want, and forcing the external world to conform to our expectations. Manipulation abuses others because it cannot accept even the possibility of disappointment. Those who manipulate are afraid that others will let them down - they are terrified of the vulnerability that comes with Faith. People turn to Manipulation because they believe that others cannot be trusted, only controlled. Manipulators assume that if they force others to do what they want, then they'll be safe from disappointment and fulfilled when they get what we want. They are terribly mistaken.

The Fruit of Manipulation

In order to treat Manipulation we must be able to recognize it and know what motivates it. Manipulation deceives us into believing we can take control of life, but in reality Manipulation only ends up controlling us. The more Manipulation we use, the more reliant we become on it. When we lose control of our emotions and actions, throw a big tantrum, and end up getting our way, we become more inclined to react similarly in the future. When this pattern takes hold, we explode when we encounter difficulty. If we get our way, we will manipulate more in the future. If we are resisted, we ramp up the tantrum. No matter what, Manipulation does not lead to intimacy or fulfillment, it only brings frustration and anger. Manipulation is ultimately a failure to love:

Whoever claims to love God yet hates a brother or sister is a liar. For whoever does not love their brother and sister, whom they have seen, cannot love God, whom they have not seen. And he has given us this command: Anyone who loves God must also love their brother and sister.
- 1 John 4:20-21 NIV

God's Word makes it clear that we can't love him if we can't also love our brothers and sisters, who have been made to reflect God's image. You cannot surrender to God while also trying to control the people who reflect him. Only love will bring us the fulfillment and intimacy we long for, but love cannot be forced or controlled. Manipulation will inevitably disappoint us regardless of whether we get what we want or not. Remember, fulfillment depends on *how* we get our desires met, not *whether* we get them met. Manipulation fails to bring us the satisfaction we hoped it would because the means spoils the reward.

Manipulation always prioritizes the gratification of desire over the quality of the relationship: i.e. a manipulator will take advantage of a relationship to get what they want. No one will linger complacently with someone who constantly manipulates. Manipulation is a one-way road that leads us to be alone and afraid - the very thing that Manipulation is working to avoid. Attempting to force others to comply, even if they would have done so willingly, pushes them away. Manipulation creates a conundrum, robbing itself of the very thing it most deeply desires: to guarantee the affection of others.

Let's review where true fulfillment comes from:

1. Self Esteem: Being yourself, and the payoff of taking a personal risk by being open and vulnerable with your desires.

2. Receiving Affection: Demonstrated in others' free-willed choices to love us.

3. Satisfied Desire: Receiving whatever it was you wanted.

Although employing manipulative tactics might get you what you want, it doesn't bring fulfillment because of what it does to the first two sources of fulfillment - ourselves and our relationships. Manipulation obscures the first source of fulfillment by focusing on controlling what others do rather than what we ourselves do. When we manipulate, we aren't taking primary action to meet our own needs. Rather, through a variety of manipulative tactics, we burden others with the responsibility of managing our desires, disappointments, and emotions.

In the 1950's, the psychologist Julian Rotter[2] created a concept to describe the difference between meeting our needs personally and expecting others to meet our needs, called an Internal or External Locus of Control. With an Internal Locus of Control, we take personal responsibility for our own wellbeing and see ourselves as in control of our own actions, thoughts, and feelings. An External Locus of Control believes that our behaviors, feelings, and needs are solely influenced by outside forces. These might be the weather, your family, the stock market, the success or failure of your favorite sports team, or anything else your wellbeing to be influenced by. An External Locus of Control can lead to a sense of being a victim or helpless. The truth likely lies somewhere in the gray area - that we both have a degree of control, and that we are influenced by external factors. Manipulation, however, assumes that the External Locus of Control is more accurate. But rather than shifting to an Internal Locus of Control, Manipulation attempts to control as many as of the external factors as it can.

Common sense tells us that we cannot make demands of forces we aren't in control of. Yet Manipulation demands that the world, which we do not control, conforms to our expectations. This is the first faulty belief that Manipulation generates: we can control what happens to us and what other people do. Differentiating what we do and do not control is paramount if we hope to address Manipulation. As the Serenity Prayer says:

> *God grant me the serenity*
> *to accept the things I cannot change;*
> *courage to change the things I can;*
> *and wisdom to know the difference.*

So what are the things we can change? Ultimately, our sphere of control is constantly changing. One person might control a multi-million dollar business empire, and another might lose control over their bodily functions. At minimum, we control a single factor - as Viktor Frankl, Holocaust survivor, wrote in his book, *Man's Search for Meaning*(3):

> *"Everything can be taken from a man but one thing: the last of the human freedoms—to choose one's attitude in any given set of circumstances, to choose one's own way."*

Everything you can control, except your attitude, can be stripped away. How you choose to respond to circumstances around you is the single thing constantly in your control. Trouble and frustration will arise when we attempt to exert control where we have none. We certainly have some influence on external factors, but thinking that things will go exactly according to our plans only sets us up to eventually feel powerless. Hoping to control that which we cannot control is a recipe for disaster. Frankl's quote helps us recognize that, while we can change our actions, we cannot control others' actions. Despite what some people may think, it is impossible to control others' decisions. Their attitude is their responsibility.

When approaching others with a desire, Manipulation makes the exchange into a battle of willpower. Manipulation tries to force the other person to respond as desired. But our responses are the sole thing we have entirely under our control. Where this strategy works, the positive feelings of Self Esteem are contorted into an ugly counterfeit: we feel an uneasy sense of pleasure at, seemingly, dictating what others do. This is not genuine Self Esteem, which is edified by being courageous. Instead, it is a fouly-dependent, easily-provoked, power trip. Manipulation creates anxiety at the onset in its objective to control that which cannot be controlled. Screaming at the sky for rain won't do us any good, but doing so anyway will create a sort of paranoia within us as the rain comes and goes as it pleases. Are we in control, or aren't we? We can no longer be sure.

Manipulation torpedos the second factor of fulfillment, Receiving Affection. From the manipulator's perspective, they can no longer discern others' free will. As we discussed, Manipulation cannot truly control others no more than screaming at the sky will cause it to rain. However, when it *does* rain, when others give in to Manipulation, it creates uncertainty in the eyes of the manipulator. Did it rain coincidentally? Or does shouting at the sky really make the heavens pour? The manipulator is unable to determine if others truly care or simply give in because they feel controlled. Ultimately, this uncertainty influences the manipulator's perception of whether or not people truly care about them. In other words, Manipulation wrestles with the doubt that others would act as desired if they were not controlled. This is an absolute, critical blow to our need to be cared for. Manipulation obscures the fulfillment that happens when we know others care for us. When we demand that someone do something for us, and then they do it, we can no longer tell what is motivating their actions - Do they truly care for us, or are they only afraid of us?

This uncertainty heightens insecurity in our relationships, and creates yet another reason Manipulation makes us anxious. Because the manipulator can no longer discern the care (or lack thereof) of others, distrust begins to settle in. Manipulators come to doubt that others will act as desired if they have the choice. So, the manipulator justifies that others must be continually manipulated into performing the desired outcome. It is a sad shadow of the relational fulfillment that we are meant for, but seemingly feels "safer." Manipulators are not willing to risk relational disappointment, and so they seek to find ever-escalating means of controlling the people around them. This means that manipulators have to constantly work harder to find ways to control other people, constantly analyzing what tactics are working. As opposed to simply being honest and allowing others to have a genuine relationship with them, manipulators sacrifice intimacy for heartless compliance.

Thus, Manipulation leads to anxiety by creating a culture of "walking on eggshells." Manipulation changes heightens tension for everyone in the relationship. As communication becomes veiled and strained, we become wary of doing or saying the wrong thing for fear that they'll lash out. Rather than simply being open and honest we become cautious, anticipating the next bout of manipulative rage, guilt, or shaming. The energy we put into tiptoeing around one another is draining, and only further mounts to the growing anxiety created by Manipulation. Inevitably, the very thing the manipulator fears will come to pass: Manipulation will fail, and others will resist or defy manipulative pressure.

Faith recognizes and accepts that we are not in control of external factors, but Manipulation believes that if it tries hard enough it can get its way. In doing so, Manipulation tries to skirt the difficulty of accepting the things that are not in our control. Manipulation fights a losing battle; it relies too heavily on controlling the external world. It seeks control where it has none, and fails to exercise the power that we actually do have: focusing on personal choices and actions. This failure bars us from the Self Esteem and Received Affection that we would otherwise experience. Instead, it leaves us either disillusioned or with a puffed-up illusion of sick power, which is really just anxiety.

Because this strategy doesn't fulfill completely even when it works, manipulators will try over and over again to squeeze every ounce of compliance out of others. In this way, gratified Manipulation is an addictive loop - the more we can manipulate our way into getting our way, the more we'll use it in the future. Not because it worked, but because only partially worked.

On the other hand, when we use Manipulation to find fulfillment and fail to do so, we face a choice: continue to be manipulative, or find some other means of searching for fulfillment. If we choose another means, we move quadrants (hopefully back to operating through Faith). When we continue in Manipulation yet give up the hope of fulfillment, Manipulation turns against the people we first sought to control.

Manipulation that fails to control others degrades into vengeance, where the manipulator seeks retribution for the supposed wrongdoings that have been done to them. When others resist being manipulated, vengeance changes the manipulator's course of action. It prompts manipulators to no longer seek the fulfillment of their original desire, but to find grim pleasure in harming the people who have thwarted them. It is no longer about getting what they want, but punishing those who defy them. At its worst, vengeance becomes abuse. Perhaps even going so far as to blame the victim: "I wouldn't have done that if you would have just listened!" This blame-shifting is only another iteration of abusive vengeance.

Even when vengeance is rather innocuous (if there is such a thing as innocuous vengeance!), there is no winning. If someone is using vengeance against you, there is nothing you can do to appease them - they have become your enemy. Consider, for example, two people arguing about how to spend their evening:

Person A: "Let's go for a walk."
Person B: "No, let's stay in and watch TV."
A: "But we did that last night, let's go for a walk."
B: "I'm too tired, let's just watch TV."
A: "Go for a walk!"
B: "Watch TV!"
A: "Walk!"
B: "TV!"
A: "Walk!"
B: "TV!"

And finally someone acquiesces:

A: "Fine. Whatever. Let's watch TV."

But it's too late. Person B has been angered and no longer cares about getting their way. All they care about is vengeance - making the other person pay for defying them.

B: "No, no, no. Let's do what *you* want. Let's go for a walk."
A: "Okay! Let's just go then!"
B: "Ohhhhh, I see. You just want to get whatever you want."

Whether walking or watching TV, Person B will make Person A suffer for arguing with them in the first place. Person B doesn't care about TV any longer. They don't want to compromise, they don't even care about winning the argument. They want Person A to grovel. Using such tactics inherently changes us. Vengeance doesn't bring us any kind of fulfillment or satisfaction. Regardless of what Person A and B decide to do, the company only brings misery so long as there is vengeance.

Manipulation, and especially vengeance, changes our focus from the prioritization of relational health to an obsession with controlling people. When others resist being controlled, vengeance steps in and further deteriorates our desire, causing our gratification to be found only in making others as miserable as we feel. But even that fails to bring the manipulator any kind of joy. These changes to our character are slow but deadly, sapping any pleasure we may have once had. It is no wonder the Proverbs say:

Better a bread crust shared in love than a slab of prime rib served in hate.
- Proverbs 15:17 MSG

In this verse, we once again see that the means of how something is obtained plays a larger role in our fulfillment than getting the "thing" itself. It is better to have next to nothing when it is obtained through Faith and love than to have much obtained through Manipulation and control. The same principle applies to how we mature throughout our lives: How we grow matters more than whether we grow.

Guilt vs. Conviction

Which is more important, do you suppose: the personal changes we desire, or the motivation for that change? As a counselor, I hear people talk about the changes that they want to make in their lives. In the past, I would plow ahead, attempting to do my best to help them attain personal growth. But I began to notice that it wasn't working as well as I supposed. Curious, I started to do more investigative work about why people were wanting to change. I found that although the changes themselves might be good, the motivation was oftentimes foul. For instance, someone might say they want to lose weight, but be motivated to do so because they want their peers to stop teasing and bullying them. The motive isn't nefarious, but it is fearful and focused on the wrong objective. Better to desire change to because of a personal belief than a feeling that's pushed on you. Personally, I believe that what motivates us to change is vastly more important than the change itself. If we change for the wrong reasons, the changes are disingenuous and are likely to be short-lived. So what are the "wrong reasons" we might change?

Of all the reasons we might change, external pressures that involve fear are perhaps the worst. Fear and desire are opposite manifestations of the same longing. Where desire propels us towards some objective, fear moves us away from the negative form of that desire. For example, one might fear rejection and desire acceptance. If we operate under the guise of desiring acceptance, then we are motivated towards that end; we will find ways to be accepted. However, if we live under the fear of rejection, no amount of acceptance dispels the fear. In fact, while living in that fear, the more acceptance we get, the more fear we will live with as we dread losing what we've obtained. Fear cannot reach an end goal.

Using fear to motivate others (or even ourselves!) is a form of Manipulation where the person is made to feel bad for being the way they are. When this kind Manipulation is overt, most people are savvy enough to know to reject it. But the more subtle it is, the harder it is to both recognize and reject. The apex of this belittling Manipulation is guilt. Guilt turns others' desire into fear, and then forms a connection from that fear to what we want them to change. Consider the example of an interaction between parent and child:

Parent: Why isn't your homework done?

Child: I dunno.

Parent: Don't you care about having a nice life when you're older?

Child: I guess so.

Parent: Well when you're grown up, who's going to buy you all those things you love so much?

Child: I will.

Parent: Not if you don't get your homework done. You won't be able to have nice things if all you ever do is sit around.

In the span of only a few seconds, this parent has taken their anxiety about their child's future and translated it into a threat: If you don't do your homework, you'll be miserable. But, paradoxically, all this does to the child is make them more resistant: They are annoyed at their parent, and are now motivated to get their homework done to merely get their parent off their back. Perhaps they even believe the message - that they must work hard to avoid future misery. Notice that the motivation is avoidance, which is based in fear. They don't know what they are working for, only what they are working to avoid. It will not bring satisfaction.

We can learn to identify guilt by uncovering and disarming its three inherent messages:

1. You are wrong.

Guilt criticizes, meaning that it blames the person and not their actions or behavior. Guilt focuses on *who* is wrong rather than on *what* is wrong. Guilt tells us we're not only messing up, but that we are messed up. Being told that you are inherently wrong implies that it isn't okay to be yourself. Guilt may communicate a message like: "Not doing your homework is the wrong thing to do," all the while ignoring the circumstances that may have caused your homework not to be done.

2. You are bad.

Guilt also tells us that we are bad; that something within us is odd, unusual, unlovely, and causes us to be outcast. Being told that "you are bad" strips us of relational security, causing us to try to conform out of a fear that we will be abandoned. Running with our example, guilt may say: "You didn't do your homework because you're lazy."

3. You better do better.

The third message guilt communicates is that we had better shape up - or else. It uses threatening words, tones, and implications to create pressure and force change. The problem with this third message is twofold. First, it uses fear to motivate, which will only work so far as we give into the fear by trying to avoid punishment. If our fear fades, so too does the motivation gleaned from guilt. Neither guilt nor fear can cultivate a lasting change, as most of us resolve to not live lives of fear. Second, and more importantly, the message of "you better do better" creates dissonance in its self-defeating message. If we give into this last message of guilt, we work hard to put on an act of fitting in, all the while fearing that we really do not. We are led to believe that we have something to prove: "Do your homework, lazy!"

Guilt, in essence, tells us two contrary messages: That we are bad and wrong, and that we must somehow do better. But, consider this: how are we supposed to do better if we're fundamentally bad and wrong? Remember, guilting messages do not convey that our actions are wrong, but that we ourselves are bad and wrong. Thus, guilt fails to foster a belief that we are capable and supported in meeting others' expectations of us. If we are told that we must do our homework, and because we're not doing it, that we're lazy, how can laziness produce results? If what I really am is lazy, then I am incapable of doing my homework. So, I either give up and prove the manipulator right, or give in and do my homework out of a motivation to prove that I'm not lazy, all the while fearing that I truly am - otherwise, I would know I have nothing to prove. Even if my homework does get done, as soon as I no longer fear judgment, my performance will slack because it wasn't an inherent desire to begin with. Guilt fails to catalyze the outcome the manipulator desires, and only produces frustration, insecurity, and faking it.

Take this example boys oftentime hear: "Man up, you wuss!" This berating tells us that, as a wuss, something about us bad and wrong. It is the connotation that we aren't masculine enough, in whatever context it applies to. While being called weak, we are simultaneously expected to "man up." But how are we supposed to "man up" if we are a "wuss?" It lays a trap for us, seeking to provoke us to defend ourselves, which really only exposes our inner insecurity. Guilt challenges our identity, and traps us as soon as we give in. When we allow these challenges to sink in, we try to "man up" while simultaneously fearing that we are really a wuss, oftentimes driving boys to pseudo-masculine behavior. When we internalize guilt, we become our own enemy - fearful that if people saw us for who we really are, we wouldn't be enough.

We are not powerless in dealing with messages of guilt, however. We can rebuke guilt and preserve the integrity of our identities. Consider how Jesus was tempted by Satan:

> *After fasting forty days and forty nights, he was hungry. The tempter came to him and said, "If you are the Son of God, tell these stones to become bread."*
> *- Matthew 4:2-3 NIV*

In this case and two other instances, Satan brought Jesus' identity into question by saying: "If you are the Son of God…" Satan tries to drive a wedge into Jesus' heart by challenging him to defend his identity. Our identity has power to shape our beliefs about our desires and our very selves. If we fall victim to this kind of challenge, it shows doubt in who we are. Jesus had no doubts about who he was:

> *Jesus answered, "It is written: 'Man shall not live on bread alone, but on every word that comes from the mouth of God.'"*
> *- Matthew 4:4 NIV*

Jesus is secure in his identity. He doesn't bother defending Himself as the Son of God even after Satan casts doubt on him. Instead, Jesus focuses on the truth. Jesus had the ability to do as Satan suggested and turn stones into bread for himself. He is not being tempted with a feat outside of his power, but he will not allow Satan to get a rise out of him. How uncharacteristic of him would it have been if he tried to prove himself: "*If I'm the Son of God, huh?! Well! You just stand there and watch! I'll make those stones into the best loaves that ever graced the Earth! Now who's the Son of God, eh?*" Trying to prove yourself to someone who is challenging, guilting, or accusing you does no good. It is a cheap trick that only makes us doubt ourselves.

These kinds of challenges crop up in scripture as one of the primary ways that Satan tries to work, as he is out to make us doubt ourselves and God. Guilt is pervasive enough that it finds its way into churches, and our own thinking. Frankly, I've likely used it myself in this very book! It is difficult, if not impossible to avoid guilt. Though, in all fairness, sin *rightly* causes us to feel guilt. But even still, that guilt does not produce repentance - only condemnation. It is God's kindness that prompts us to repent and to change. Whenever we hear the "ought to" voice we are being subjected to guilt, as though you were being forced to do something you don't really want to do:

"I ought to pray more."

"We need to go to church."

"You have to forgive them."

These "ought to" messages subtly imply: "Something's wrong with you. You're a fake, but can't let anyone see it. You have to do better if you want to be good." It's an easy pill to swallow. The aforementioned examples - prayer, church, and forgiveness - are all good things, but what motivates us to those things is *more* important. Which would you rather have: someone who mindlessly professes to "love" you because they're afraid of what you'd do if they didn't love you, or someone who loves you because they freely choose to? Using guilt may create behavioral obedience, but it fails to draw the heart to love. I think it's fair to say that God desires people who pray, attend church, and forgive, not because it's what they are forced to do, but because it's what they want to do. We are meant to be people of conviction, not of guilt.

Conviction is the alternative form of motivation, and it is contrary to guilt in every way. Conviction is a belief that grips us in our innermost being, our heart. Yet, paradoxically, convictions are oftentimes difficult to discern. It whispers messages of goodness and love, and offers us invitations. Conviction says:

1. You are good.

When God created mankind, he saw us and called us good. Although we know that the sinful nature is bad and naturally draws us to feel guilt, being born again as a Christian grants us a new nature. This new self, the new heart, is one that God calls good, and is solely due to Christ (Romans 8:9-11). Knowing that we are good helps us to know that it is okay for us to be our true selves - the person that God made us to be. God sees past our faults and brokenness, perceiving our hearts.

2. You are loved.

Guilt communicates that we are unlovable and therefore must change in order to earn love, but conviction says that we are loved just the way we are. We are meant to live in the security of God's unconditional love for us. If we doubt God's love, scripture answers us definitively:

But God demonstrates his own love for us in this: While we were still sinners, Christ died for us.

- Romans 5:8 NIV

Greater love has no one than this: to lay down one's life for one's friends.
- John 15:13 NIV

Christ laid down his life for us while we were still covered in our guilt and sin. He does not wait to love us until we are perfect.

Thus, these first two messages of conviction, that we are good and that we are loved, establishes us in personal and relational security. In other words, any change motivated by conviction is not powered by judgments, threats, or challenges, but kindness. We know that change is not necessary, because only one thing is needed - the grace offered to us by Christ - and that has nothing to do with our own effort. Knowing that our hearts are good and that we are loved readies us to hear the third message of conviction:

3. There is something better.

This message points us toward a different, "better" course of action compared to what we are currently doing. It invites us to something different without any judgment. The tricky part is that no one has successfully replicated the ability to convey this message as the Spirit of God does. If I am convinced there is a better way to do something, no amount of insisting will make someone else feel the same conviction that I do. Their convictions are their own despite my instance. Therefore, using Manipulation to reach an objective I consider to be good is folly.

Luckily, when we stop trying to manipulate and instead begin to live out of our convictions, we begin to live in freedom. At the same time, as we cease trying to manipulate others, we create space for others to also live out of their own convictions. In other words, if we manipulate others to do what is right, rather than learning what is right, they only learn to manipulate. If we focus on living by our convictions, others learn to live by their own convictions. Note that I am not advocating for passivity in the face of evil, but self-control and grace in a world obsessed with power.

Observe what Paul says about people who disagree about their convictions regarding food:

For the kingdom of God is not a matter of eating and drinking, but of righteousness, peace and joy in the Holy Spirit, because anyone who serves Christ in this way is pleasing to God and approved by men. Let us therefore make every effort to do what leads to peace and to mutual edification. Do not destroy the work of God for the sake of food. All food is clean, but it is wrong for a man to eat anything that causes someone else to stumble.
- Romans 14:17-20 NIV (emphasis added)

Whether you have convictions about food, television, holidays, or anything else, what matters most is following your convictions from Faith and loving other people well. Paul supposes that, rather than trying to convince or push your convictions onto others, living peaceably with others is more important. It astounds me that the Spirit is able to communicate convictions to us free of any guilt. It is no wonder the Spirit must reside within us. For if not, if conviction were to come from some external source, we would be back under the old testament law. But because conviction comes from the gentle whispering of the Spirit of God within us, it can oftentimes be drowned out by the loud voice of guilt.

Living by conviction is not as flashy or dramatic as living in guilt. In fact, convictions can easily be ignored. If you are told at work, "You've not been pulling your weight around here. You really need to step up your effort." You might feel remorse, shame, or pressure to work harder. Likely, you would have some fear even after making changes. If instead you were struck by the conviction: "I've been doing alright at work, but it would be good if I put in more effort," I doubt you would go home and stew about it the same way. However, that conviction may not bring about any change - you may simply think that it's a good thought, pat yourself on the back, and continue on as you were. However if that conviction *does* lead to change, the effort is genuine. Although it may produce the same observable results as being guilted, conviction will bring about different personal results. You would feel proud about your results rather than fearing additional criticism.

A real life example I had with this occurred about a month ago. For the past few weeks, I had been spending my leisure time rereading one of my favorite fictions. I was enjoying it, but I began to notice an unsettled feeling crop up when I continued to read. The feeling was easy to brush off, and I didn't pay it much attention. One day I read a chapter before putting the book down to get some work done. Later, when I finished my work, I thought about picking the book back up again. Only this time I paused to consider what that nagging feeling was. Almost immediately my thoughts went to how I hadn't gotten much out of rereading the book. I also recognized that I wanted to finish it, but had to agree that I didn't feel edified by the book. My mind then drifted to a copy of C.S. Lewis' classics sitting on my bedside table, and how I hadn't read it in a while. Seizing the thread of conviction, I decided to read Lewis' work. It was exactly what I had been looking for, and felt very much *right*. I still ended up finishing the fictional book too!

If this story taught me anything it was that convictions are gentle, whispered invitations. They may be hard to discern, but when we follow our convictions we become more apt to respond according to our desires and the stirrings of God. Following our convictions is but one way to manage the pressure that Manipulation puts on us. If we desire freedom from forces that seek to trap us in Manipulation, ultimately we must find our way back into Faith. Meaning, we must come face to face with the painful reality that we cannot make life, other people, or God predictable.

From Manipulation to Faith

Manipulation is the result of what happens when we seek to take control of situations or people which are inherently out of our grasp. Choosing to give into Manipulation diverts our focus from naming and communicating our desires to seeking fulfillment through control. When others give way to that control, all Manipulation rewards us with is anxiety, because there isn't any certainty as to what led to our "fulfillment." For instance, anxiety from Manipulation may make us wonder: Did God answer my prayer because he wanted to, or because I framed my prayer in just the right way? Manipulation that gets its way cannot tell apart a cooperative achievement from a coerced achievement. That anxiety then compels us to manipulate all the more for fear that if we did not, we won't continue to find fulfillment - not realizing that fulfillment has already been compromised. The great lie of Manipulation is that it can help you obtain fulfillment, when in reality it causes us to continually live in tension and disappointment. Thus, when Manipulation is resisted, all the pent up frustration comes boiling over - incorrectly holding others accountable for our peevishness.

However, we need not turn to vengeance when we inevitably face disappointment in life. If we are willing to linger in the tension of disappointment without giving way to vengeful outbursts, we can make the choice to return to living in Faith by trusting God. Ultimately, Manipulation is a refusal to acknowledge and be hurt by disappointment. So, when we pause to accept that there are things we cannot control, Manipulation loses its power. Furthermore, seeking closeness with God in the midst of disappointment reorients our priorities. Our desires slowly change from whatever they were, to a longing for God.

Recently, my wife came home from a MOPS gathering with a plastic cup that had the NIRV version of Romans 12:12 printed on it. It read:

"When you are suffering, be patient."

For whatever reason, reading that sentence stated just a smidge differently made me realize the brilliance of the passage. This thought is completely backwards from what most of us do when we are hurting. In the midst of suffering, we focus on and hope for the quickest alleviation of our suffering. We want the pain to go away as fast as possible. In direct contradiction to this, scripture urges us to be patient when we are suffering, to take a moment to pause when we are hurting.

This seems counter-intuitive. Why on earth would we be encouraged to linger in pain? I won't pretend to have the complete answer, though I believe there are some observations we can make:

Only a few verses later in Romans 12:19 NIV, Paul writes:

Do not take revenge, my friends, but leave room for God's wrath, for it is written: "It is mine to avenge; I will repay," says the Lord.

If God calls us to let go of vengeance so that he can take care of it, then perhaps he also wants us to let him be in control of our healing. Oftentimes what people think will help them to feel better, in fact, does not. I don't mean to imply that it's wrong to do things for our wellbeing. If you're in physical pain, by all means, do something about it. What we're talking about is the demand or insistence that discomfort (especially nonphysical discomfort), *must* go away. By trying to rush through our suffering, we might be trying to manipulate something we do not have control over.

When we cannot manage our pain on our own, we make it worse by anxiously trying to make it go away. Suffering is only compounded when we think something will help us, and then we find that nothing has changed or that we are even worse off. When we patiently lean on God in the midst of suffering and surrender our urgency, we stop exacerbating our suffering needlessly and gain intimacy with God. Trusting God when we are suffering is not about trying to earn his favor, hoping that he will do what we want if we act good enough. To do so would only be another iteration of Manipulation in the form of bargaining.

Manipulation believes that God is untrustworthy and therefore must be somehow manipulated into doing what we want. As if that were possible! By being patient when we are disappointed, we accept the outcome and cease compounding our suffering by trying to force a way out. Instead, when we seek God while we are hurting we return home to Faith - bringing our heartfelt requests to our Father without controlling the outcome. Faith is the ultimate declaration that we believe God is good and trustworthy, and this sentiment is made all the more definitive when we choose Faith in the midst of suffering.

Scripture: *"When you are suffering, be patient." - Romans 12:12 NIRV*

Thought: Manipulation is a self-defense mechanism we use to control others when we feel we cannot trust them. When we use Manipulation we will either become anxious or vengeful, and even more likely to Manipulate in the future. God calls us to return to Faith by trusting in him when we are suffering.

Questions:

- What situations cause you to use Manipulation?
- How have you been subjected to others' Manipulation?
- What are we called to do when we find ourselves suffering?

Chapter 4

GREED

What causes fights and quarrels among you? Don't they come from your desires that battle within you? You desire but do not have, so you kill. You covet but you cannot get what you want, so you quarrel and fight. You do not have because you do not ask God.

- James 4:1-2 NIV

Desire without knowledge is not good, and whoever makes haste with his feet misses his way.

- Proverbs 19:2 ESV

Scratching the Itch

A couple of years ago I helped my father-in-law with some yard work, mostly pruning limbs on some overgrown trees. I spent a great deal of time tromping through the woods, pulling away brambles and vines so that we could get close to the trees with our saws. The next morning I woke up scratching an itch that wouldn't seem to go away. Apparently I had gotten poison oak oil on my gloves and as I worked I spread it to my clothes and, eventually, onto my skin. My clothing and shoes I wore that day had to be bagged and thrown out. I had blistering rashes that covered about a third of my body, all up and down my arms, legs, neck, and chest. What was worse, none of the over-the-counter remedies seemed to do anything. I eventually had to go to the doctor and was prescribed an ointment.

While I was supposed to apply it twice a day, at morning and night, I found it to be bothersome. Most mornings I'd find myself stubbornly sitting on the couch and resisting the urge to scratch, but also not willing to get up and put on my ointment. My problems really started when the itch became too much to bear. Just thinking about it now makes me itch all over! But rather than applying my prescription as I should have, I'd give in and scratch. The relief was immediate, or so I thought. After only a few seconds, the blasted itch would return. Well, by this point my resistance was null - I'd go right back to scratching. If given enough time, I'd be scratching without stop; not so much to make the itch go away, but to keep from feeling the itch in the first place. I wound up scratching myself bloody. Only then would I get up off the couch and go apply my ointment, chastising myself.

The strange thing about it was that even after my rash and the itch was gone, I'd still scratch. I didn't even notice I was doing it until my wife said something. What happened? How did I go from resisting an itchy rash, to scratching even when the itch was gone? Scratching had become habitual; it was like an addiction. Scripture frequently refers to addiction as being enslaved or mastered:

> *"I have the right to do anything," you say—but not everything is beneficial. "I have the right to do anything"—but I will not be mastered by anything.*
> *- 1 Corinthians 6:12 NIV*

I had the freedom to scratch the itch or to apply my ointment. No one forced me to do one or the other. But the freedom to choose doesn't mean we are also free of the consequences of our choices. And some choices have the consequence of inhibiting our ability to objectively choose. Said differently, the more we choose something, the more likely we are to choose it in the future. We can become mastered - scratching even after the itch is gone.

My trial with poison oak was really about my struggle for independence, where *I* tried to set my own precedent on fulfillment without relying on anyone or anything else. I believed that I could manage the itch by myself.

I didn't heed the wisdom of my doctor. I didn't listen to my wife telling me to go put on my ointment. I just sat and scratched. This kind of behavior, where we take stubborn, independent action for our own fulfillment, is the third of the Forging Character Quadrants, known as Greed.

Greed is distinguished from the other quadrants by the lack of regard it has for others. It takes other people and even God for granted, focusing only on one's sense of entitlement regardless of how others are impacted. Greed is not the same thing as self-care, however. For instance, I do not have to ask or even involve anyone else in making lunch for myself. We are not greedy for taking care of our basic needs. In fact, it is good for us to have some level of autonomy. Being carelessly and overly dependent on others also wouldn't be considerate. Greed is entirely self-absorbed and thinks only about our own gratification.

For example, perhaps I think that my sandwich wasn't *just* right. I heedlessly consider it to be ruined and toss it, clueless of the waste. On the other hand, when I recognize the gift that my sandwich truly is and how privileged I am to be eating it, my focus changes. I come to recognize the sun, rain, soil, plants, people, animals, and the God who made my sandwich possible that I might enjoy it in that moment.

Gratitude is an increasingly difficult perspective to have. As our society gears itself more towards instant gratification free of consequence, we take life for granted more and more. I recently played a video game, and the experience was much different from when I was a kid. There are so many details I didn't notice as a child: the logic algorithms running the game coded by a programmer, the symphonic score which had to be composed, performed, and recorded, the small sounds of nature which had to be captured in real life, and the story I knew was written and revised by professional story developers. It was almost overwhelming to consider how much work had gone into making the game. As I played, I found myself experiencing a different kind of enjoyment, much more rooted in gratitude than in thrill-seeking.

However, it is not enough to solely recognize what others have done for us. In order to not be greedy we must also respect others' rights. It may be appropriate for me to make myself lunch, but if I stole the ingredients, I've taken it too far. Similarly, a child might say "thank you," while they take something right out of your hands without asking. Their words do little to assuage the fact that they just took something from you! Mere recognition of others' feelings and rights won't cut it. We must honor others by balancing our needs and theirs. Our focus, whether placed on our own gratification or on how to love others, determines where our fulfillment stems from.

If our motivation is to love more deeply, our desires mature us as we grow beyond immature egocentrism. Conversely, desire that lacks recognition and respect for others never really satisfies us. Consider the difference between someone who serves at a homeless shelter to give back to others, versus someone who serves at a homeless shelter to only prove that they are a good person. The latter individual will walk away unsatisfied because their heart is in the wrong place. They're doing "good" things but their focus is selfish. Fulfillment is denied them because they are too caught up in themselves.

Greed has utter disregard for others' contributions and rights because it is too consumed with gratifying the self. Similar to Manipulation, Greed is a tactic we use to self-protect from disappointment by vowing to ourselves never to rely on or need anyone else. We find all kinds of excuses to justify greedy behavior, such as maintaining the belief that, "everyone is only out for themselves, and so you can't blame me for taking care of number one!" And, while this trend is changing, we still idolize celebrities and characters that supposedly exemplify total independence. Dependency doesn't mean we're weak, it means we have the strength to own up to the reality that we cannot live life on our own. Need I remind: we are meant to rely on God - otherwise, Faith counts for nothing. But acknowledging our dependency feels vulnerable. Thus, Greed baits us with the promise that we can be stronger by taking whatever we want whenever we want it without involving anyone else, and that it will work out just fine. "I can do it on my own." While it is a relief to know that we aren't meant to be able to do it all on our own, that reality all but unacceptable to those in Greed.

Greed refuses to trust God and others with personal desires, instead seeking gratification on its own terms. As a means of trying to find fulfillment, Greed is characterized by taking. Greed tries to take whatever it wants without relying on anyone because it fears others will only disappoint us. But to imagine that we can achieve fulfillment with complete independence is foolishness. Obtaining the objects of our desires through Greed doesn't bring fulfillment, as fulfillment is contingent upon Self Esteem (gained through vulnerability), Receiving Affection (from others' involvement), and (most insignificantly) Satisfied Desire. Greed limits the most important aspects of fulfillment because it excludes others and refuses to risk vulnerability. Instead, all Greed leaves us with are poorly obtained crumbs.

Greed takes the risk of being vulnerable and replaces it with a different risk: the violation of rules, laws, or others' boundaries to find selfish gratification. Consider, for example, someone who breaks into a house to steal a television so that they can watch TV. Because Greed only considers selfish gratification, it has no qualms about others' rights. Rather, the only concern regarding others' boundaries is what might happen if they are caught. The tension this creates is similar to a gambler's high, imparting a rush of adrenaline for a relatively small payoff. Gratification of desire through Greed is not as significant as the fulfillment found in Faith. It is a big risk for a small reward.

Whenever desire is gratified through using Greed, it will only temporarily alleviate the ache of desire without fulfilling it completely. Since Greed is a *self* derived means of finding fulfillment, when the desire inevitably returns, we will be driven to simply take more. After all, it seems like we are the ones in control. A cycle is eventually created: mounting tension as desire builds, gambling by crossing boundaries to selfishly gratify the desire, a brief but intense alleviation, and repeat. This cycle quickly creates an addictive pattern. It doesn't matter what the desire is, or what the gratification looks like - addiction will manifest wherever Greed is allowed to run the show.

Imagine being hungry and there being only two different meals you can choose between. One meal you can prepare and eat yourself, and requires little-to-no work. However, this meal is also looked upon poorly by others and people are negatively judged for eating it. The second meal requires cooperation to prepare, and can only be eaten in the company of others who may or may not choose to eat with you. After working to prepare the second meal, you try to eat it, but feel uncertain about the other people with you. Will they join you or not? Frustrated at the uncertainty and difficulty, you try the first meal instead. At first, it's everything you hoped it would be, and comforts your feelings of hunger and loneliness.

However, no sooner have you finished that you realize you are, in fact, hungry all over again. Confused, you take more of the first meal, thinking that perhaps you didn't eat enough. But the problem persists. As soon as you stop eating, your hunger quickly returns. What's worse, you realize that you have been eating alone, which has done nothing to truly deal with your feelings of loneliness. But it also occurs to you that now you have eaten the first meal, those eating the second meal would *surely* reject you if they knew what you had done. You suppose that you cannot return to the second meal. Feeling guilty and miserable - you return to the one place you think will help you feel better - the first meal. More and more you eat. Eventually, you never cease eating; not because you are trying to be satisfied, but because you know that as soon as you stop eating, the hunger will return. All the while, you live in fear of being found out. The only salve for that fear is the food, which roundaboutly only makes the fear worse.

This is what it's like to live in Greed. When we give ourselves to Greed, we substitute waiting and trusting God with our desires for cheap knockoffs that only satisfy us temporarily. We have good, God-given desires, but when we hand them over to Greed we sabotage the relational and spiritual opportunities that desire was designed to provide. The relational value of desire is in deepening intimacy, which is found when we trust others with the most vulnerable parts of ourselves, and they open themselves to us as well. But somewhere along the way our trust can be broken. Maybe life didn't turn out the way we thought it would or someone we trusted betrayed us. The disappointment we feel when trust is broken can make it tempting to never again risk being vulnerable with others. It can feel as though we are caught between two dangers: the risk of rejection and the risk of loneliness.

The pitfall of Greed is that it causes us to fall into the trap of trying to meet our desires on our own. Under the guise of self-preservation, Greed reduces the reciprocal "give-and-take" found in healthy relationships, to solely taking what we want. But we cannot fulfill our heart's truest longings by excluding others. At best, all Greed can offer are counterfeits of the fulfillment we truly long for, which only tease our desires. This always leaves us feeling empty as our true longings can only be met in the context of trusting, intimate relationships.

Because we control the inflow of gratification when we use Greed, we open ourselves to greater and greater amounts of the object of our Greed. We eat more, exercise more, read more romance novels, view more pornography, or drink more. But we're barking up the wrong tree. The eater wants solace and looks to pie to provide it. The runner wants the admiration of others, the reader desires to be in a captivating relationship, the pornography viewer wants pleasure, and the drinker wants to stop hurting. All of these are legitimate needs taken to illegitimate places. So what happens when we realize that no matter how much we take, so long as we are in Greed, we will never find what we are looking for?

Scratching Denied

A young teenager and his father were sitting in my office. The father had just laid out the source of a conflict they had: a week ago, the son had asked his dad for something and was told no. Later that evening, the boy found his father's wallet, went online, bought what he wanted with his dad's credit card, and shipped it to a friend's house. The friend's parents then found the package once it was delivered, asked their son what was going on. The friend spilled the beans, and the jig was up. So now here they were in counseling.

The teen's actions were very obviously characterized by Greed - taking what he wanted despite breaking numerous rules. Personally, I thought the boy was fortunate to be caught, lest the problem become even worse. But I don't think the kid saw it that way. Rather, he was feeling humiliated and frustrated. He made a mistake, and he *still* didn't have what he wanted in the first place.

After sitting sullenly and quietly while his father relayed the story, he finally spoke up. He turned to his father and said something to the effect of: "None of this would have happened if *you* wouldn't have left your wallet out!"

What would you say to this young man? What words would help him to understand his actions and soothe his embarrassment? Getting caught in Greed puts us into dire straits. To find our way out, it's going to take a careful examination of the way that Greed operates, and how it ultimately fails us. First, let's consider how the denial of gratification might happen.

There are two general ways Greed can be thwarted: either the individual realizes that their Greed has been insufficient to satisfy them and turns to some other strategy, or some other person or factor bars their way to gratification.

People are unlikely to realize that their addictions are poor providers of fulfillment until they hit rock bottom, until the moment when their addiction has cost them so much that they can no longer deny that it is a problem. At such moments, we may realize that our ongoing addiction is no longer about trying to obtain fulfillment, but instead the only thing we know to keep ourselves from feeling the ache of desire. We're scratching not because we itch, but to keep the itch away. If that awareness dawns on the addict, they may realize the futility of their addiction.

The other means of inhibiting Greed happens when influence from an outside factor bars the addict's way. Maybe the addict is caught or they simply run out of whatever they were addicted to. A caring person might confront the addict or remove the object of their addiction if they are able to do so. Additionally, external pressure can be put on an addict by social pressure, morality, or laws.

External pressure alone is rarely significant enough to curb an addiction. If a morally and lawfully perfect society existed, all we would need to say is, "this thing is bad," and no one would use it. Or perhaps there wouldn't even exist any reason for laws whatsoever - people would simply not do whatever we all knew to be bad. But this obviously isn't the case, being told something is bad is not enough for us to avoid it. Even *believing* that something is bad will not stop us. Here's what Paul has to say on the matter:

> *For I know that good itself does not dwell in me, that is, in my sinful nature. For I have the desire to do what is good, but I cannot carry it out. For I do not do the good I want to do, but the evil I do not want to do—this I keep on doing.*
>
> *- Romans 7:18-19 NIV*

There is something broken within mankind. We know the good we ought to do, yet we do the opposite. We take good desires and take them to bad places. That is precisely what happens with our addictions. We take our desires for community, intimacy, delight, and pleasure to the wrong outlets. So, when this conundrum is brought to light, when Greed fails to provide fulfillment either by our own realization or when it is exposed by others, we experience guilt and condemnation. But those negative feelings only happen when we continue to stay in Greed. That is, even after exposure, we remain fixated on ourselves.

When Greed is denied fulfillment, it will often cause guilt and self-contempt. This is loathing that is directed towards oneself. Interestingly, self-contempt can also become so great that we try to pin the guilt somewhere else by blame-shifting. Even though we might protest our innocence by blaming someone else, it doesn't change the internal guilt we feel overwhelmed by. It is a good thing to be able to take responsibility for the inevitable mistakes that we will make in life. However, self-contempt takes it to an unhealthy level, admonishing, "I can't do anything right!" in addition to self put-downs: "I'm such a failure. A good-for-nothing idiot!" Why do we chastise ourselves so aggressively? Many would never even dare to speak to others the way they speak to themselves. I believe it is, in part, due to a bargain we try to make. Something like: "If I weren't such an idiot, this wouldn't have happened." We cannot change what happened in the past, and so all we can seemingly do is hope that if we berate ourselves enough, we won't repeat our same mistakes.

However, the verbal self-flagellation only serves to increase the amount of guilt and suffering we experience. And what do we know of addicts who are experiencing discomfort? They return back to the illegitimate places they think will comfort them. We go right back to the addiction that caused us to feel self-contempt in the first place, inevitably repeating the same mistakes. The guilt increases exponentially from there, as we find ourselves caught in a cycle of addiction and self-loathing. It reminds me of the verse:

> *As a dog returns to its vomit, so fools repeat their folly.*
> *- Proverbs 26:11 NIV*

Self-contempt is a trap similar to addiction, but instead of imprisoning us in problematic behaviors, self-contempt imprisons us in problematic beliefs. We erroneously come to believe that our desires only get us into trouble, that God is getting fed up with us, and that we are our own worst enemies. In truth, God patiently waits for us to trust him, our true hearts are good, and our enemies are *The* Enemy, our fallen nature, and the broken world. The reality is complex. We are both part of the problem and part of the solution.

> *Now if I do what I do not want to do, it is no longer I who do it, but it is sin living in me that does it.*
>
> *So I find this law at work: Although I want to do good, evil is right there with me. For in my inner being I delight in God's law; but I see another law at work in me, waging war against the law of my mind and making me a prisoner of the law of sin at work within me. What a wretched man I am! Who will rescue me from this body that is subject to death? Thanks be to God, who delivers me through Jesus Christ our Lord!*
>
> *- Romans 7:20-25a NIV*

A Costly Covering

We are held captive by sin and Greed, finding that we are unable to do the good we want to do. We need a savior to free us from Greed, namely, Christ. Rather than leading us to the self-contempt Greed creates when we feel guilty, Jesus frees us from our inability to do good. He pursues us even when we are back to lapping up our vomit, with grace in his eyes. Christ gives us his perfection without asking that we earn it. He permits us room to try our best, fail, and be okay in the failure because the failure no longer defines us - he does.

Once we are in Christ, we are able to perceive our old way of life with honesty, observing where we fell astray from God. Christ breaks the mold of Greed by inviting us to bring our desires to him instead of to our addictions. For me, this invitation has been one of the most breathtaking and consistent of my faith journey. Your Heavenly Father, your Savior, and the Holy Spirit - the God of the Universe, Creator of Everything - wants *you* to ask him for what you want. It's not pious. It doesn't even have to feel holy. So long as it's reflective of you:

"For You do not delight in sacrifice, or I would bring it; You take no pleasure in burnt offerings. My sacrifice, O God, is a broken spirit; a broken and contrite heart you, God, will not despise."

- Psalm 51:17 NIV

The point is not about getting what you asked for. This isn't a prosperity gospel. The point is that Jesus cares about what you care about. Do you live like you believe that? This belief fundamentally changes the way that we see God and ourselves. God is no longer the unapproachable deity that will smite you for the smallest misstep; you are no longer the screw-up living in fear.

Have you ever tried to woo someone? Maybe you tried to get closer with a friend, someone you were mentoring, a crush, or one of your children. I'll make you a promise here and now: you cannot manage it unless you show that you care or are at least interested in the things they are interested in. It doesn't mean you have to like what they like, only that you are interested in something because they are. Ask yourself: of the people that are truly close to you, how many refuse to talk to you about what excites you? I'd be equally shocked and saddened if anyone in your inner circle treated you that way. You will not believe God truly cares about you until you believe he cares about the longings you hold. But how can God care about our desires when our desires have gotten us into trouble? The secret is that when you boil our desires down, they're always the same - they just sometimes get used in the wrong way. God authored our desires to bring us closer to him - not further away.

In this new way of being, our desires become rewired. Searching for fulfillment is no longer about our gratification, but about learning to grow in intimacy with God as we trust him. When we find ourselves filled with desire, we can choose to look for fulfillment by turning towards God or away from him. Greed occurs when we make the decision to prioritize our fulfillment above our relationship with God. Relying on God feels vulnerable, especially when we doubt whether God will really come through. Regardless, God asks us to trust him even when all the evidence looks like things are going to end horribly. Even in this task, we will fail. We'll look for the "safe" alternatives to trusting God. We've failed at it since the beginning:

"Then the eyes of both of them were opened, and they realized they were naked; so they sewed fig leaves together and made coverings for themselves. Then the man and his wife heard the sound of the LORD God as he was walking in the garden in the cool of the day, and they hid from the LORD God among the trees of the garden."

- Genesis 3:7-8 NIV

After eating the forbidden fruit, Adam and Eve felt guilty and afraid, so they covered themselves and made a pitiful attempt to hide from God. They doubt God's goodness, fearing his wrath at their mistake. They do not trust God when they've blown it, like a child lying to cover their mistake because they're afraid of upsetting their parents. Their actions reveal that they do not think God will be kind with them. When Adam and Eve are inevitably confronted by God, they shirk responsibility and shift the blame. Adam even goes so far as blaming God himself!

God tells them the repercussions of their actions: Adam, Eve, and the serpent are cursed. Adam and Eve lose their place in the Garden and are given a death sentence. Following the curses, God casts Adam and Eve from Eden and bars the way for them to return. They now face a wild, unruly, and dangerous world - all the while armed with nothing more than their fig leaves and guilty consciences. I'd wager that most addicts feel similar when they're caught in their addiction.

But God has more up his sleeve. Just before being sent out of the Garden, God does something remarkable:

The LORD God made garments of skin for Adam and his wife and clothed them.

- Genesis 3:21 NIV

I can't tell you how many times I've read this verse and skimmed right past it without a second thought. This might seem like an unremarkable verse, but God is up to something profound. Remember that Adam and Eve tried to cover up their sin with fig leaves, hiding, and blame-shifting. They fail to take responsibility for their actions. In comparison, God goes to extreme lengths in dealing with their sin and nakedness. Whereas Adam and Eve made a covering of itchy fig leaves, God made them superior "garments of skin." Have you ever considered where those garments had to have come from?

I was in my mid-20's the first time I saw an animal being skinned. I took my grandfather's rifle with me to visit a good friend of mine on his family's farm in the hills of southern Indiana. We hunted for rabbits behind the garden, where they liked to nibble on the vegetables. When I eventually managed to shoot one of the rabbits, my friend's grandfather used my small pocket knife and set about cleaning the carcass. I'll spare you the details, but suffice to say that it was a gruesome sight. As I watched the old man's practiced hand I realized how in-over-my-head I would have been if I had been left to the task. But even for all his skill, "cleaning" the rabbit was anything but clean. I found that evening's dinner of fried rabbit hard to enjoy. I felt too keenly aware of the life that had been coursing through this animal only hours before. A life I was responsible for ending. It was a profoundly humbling experience, and made me realize how often I take meat for granted.

I doubt Adam and Eve ever took their new clothing for granted. To be clothed in garments of skin, some innocent creature had to die. Consider that up to this point in the Bible, death has not entered the story - no being has yet died. This is the first blood to be drawn since the beginning of Creation. Even though the lifeblood of this animal is on Adam and Eve's hands, they weren't the ones wielding the skinning knife. Adam and Eve's mistake took more than a fig leaf to fix, but God doesn't order them to do the killing. God himself kills and skins some animal whose hide was large enough to clothe a full grown man and woman.

God then fashions clothing from the skin and offers it to them as a covering for the sin and shame they brought about. I wonder if they watched God kill and skin this animal just as I watched my friend's grandpa. Did they feel the humbling weight of responsibility? What did they think as they felt the warm skin and fur of what was only moments ago a living, breathing creature that Adam had once named? They are literally comforted and clothed in death. As horrifying as this act was, God uses it as an illustration of what is to come: an innocent death and subsequent covering that makes amends for the shame brought about by sin. Sound familiar?

Looking back, Adam and Eve were rather pitiful in their attempt to atone for their sin. God, on the other hand, shows the severe cost of sin and the lengths he is willing to go to make amends. To make a suitable covering for the repercussions of their mistake, the life of an innocent animal is expended. This atonement is insufficient to entirely resolve the penalty of their sin. Their guilt, shame, and fear of vulnerability still remains. Their covering accomplishes the purpose of pointing ahead to the final atonement of the Messiah.

For all of you who were baptized into Christ have clothed yourselves with Christ.

- Galatians 3:27 NIV

Blessed are those whose transgressions are forgiven, whose sins are covered.
- Romans 4:7 NIV

God gave Adam and Eve a temporary covering through an animal's skin, but he uses it to foreshadow the work of Christ. Jesus sacrificed his life for our sake and became the final covering, the complete atonement for sin. His blood absolves our guilt and removes our shame and fear forever. Just like the innocent animal in Genesis 3, Christ took upon himself the consequences for our sins. He became our garment of righteousness, exchanging his innocent life for our guilt.

Yet, had Jesus merely died for our sins and not risen, we would still be left in guilt. How could we not be? The blood of the savior would be on our hands.

Imagine if someone died for you in the present day. An innocent passerby leaps in front of you, taking a bullet that was headed towards your heart. They save your life by giving theirs. It is a debt that you can never repay. The sacrifice of Christ is even more so. But then consider if the stranger picks themselves off the ground and reveals that they somehow are not dead, and only narrowly escaped it. The gift of their life being laid down remains, but now the debt is lifted.

Similarly, Jesus frees us from this impossible debt through his resurrection. In a one-two knockout, Jesus pays the penalty for our sin once and for all by his death, and frees us from our guilt by his return to life. Jesus' atonement and resurrection allows us to move forward confidently with trust and vulnerability, because we have no shame to hide nor debt to repay. We are under grace, not condemnation. This means that, with God, we can continue to become better people despite our setbacks or failures. Being clothed in Christ's sacrifice and life allows us to learn from our mistakes instead of being condemned by them.

Conversely, if we try to handle our mistakes without God's help, we will be unable to handle our desires and disappointments appropriately - we will inevitably give into the greedy alternatives. We will fall victim to desire gone awry, driving us to doubt God and turn to lesser idols. In our fear and shame, we avoid dealing with the real issues just as Adam and Eve did by hiding and blaming. This is a trap we are unable to free ourselves from.

We cannot manage our core desires on our own; we were never meant to. Attempting to satiate core desires such as companionship on your own is a recipe for disaster. Our core desires were meant to exist and find fulfillment within an intimate relationship with God. Everything else will fail to satisfy us; these are the very things that Greed clings to with a deathgrip. Through Greed, the desires that were once meant to bring delight now brings heartache.

The covering of Jesus, offered through the atonement of the cross, frees us from the shame of our sin and his resurrection frees us from the guilt of his blood. We are free to live, once more bringing our desires to God through Faith.

We clothe ourselves with Jesus by accepting his atonement for our sins, which is given with love, free of guilt. He is our permanent garment, completely freeing us from sin and shame. By clothing ourselves in the Lord, we can hope more fully, trust more boldly, and return to Faith.

Jealousy

As we come to trust God with our desires, our enemy can lay traps for us that cause us to doubt ourselves. One of the most brutal traps is jealousy or envy. Most Christians intuitively know that jealousy is something that is frowned upon. Scripture cautions:

But if you are bitterly jealous and there is selfish ambition in your heart, don't cover up the truth with boasting and lying. For jealousy and selfishness are not God's kind of wisdom. Such things are earthly, unspiritual, and demonic. For wherever there is jealousy and selfish ambition, there you will find disorder and evil of every kind.

- James 3:14-16 NLT

Saying that's a stern warning is a bit of an understatement. Many Christians are so sensitive to the issue, in fact, that any desire is quickly done away with for fear that it could be too jealous or ambitious. We react to our desires as though we've caught a disease. However, our fleshly sin and the wiles of the enemy cannot create some "new" problem. Jealousy is less like a disease, and more like leaving the faucet running. Temptation and sin are distortions of the genuine article. Thus, jealousy is not a new desire that must be entirely cast off, but only a good desire operating in a fashion that it wasn't meant to. By bringing jealous, ambitious, and envious desires back under the authority of Christ, our true desires (the desires that our enemy absolutely does not want us to follow) are distilled.

Jealousy cannot exist in isolation. By its very nature, jealousy can only distort a desire that is experienced in a relationship with someone or something else - i.e. you want what someone else has. But I have found that God can use these instances to wake us up to a desire he intends for us to have, under his authority of course.

The other day I was browsing homes for sale in my area. I was scrolling through when I found it - an amazing home like my wife and I have always dreamed of owning. Then I looked at the price tag, and my stomach clenched. The thought hit me like a freight train: "I'll never be able to afford something like that."

What do we do when "reality checks" squash our dreams? In my case, I had to remind myself of my true desire. It isn't for the dream home, as nice as it might be. It's for Heaven - the perfect home that God is preparing uniquely for you and I. How easy it is to lose sight of that. We settle for the lesser things, rather than endure and long for the real deal. We fantasize and covet. We demand that Earth becomes Heaven. We're like exiled princes and princesses, draping our cardboard boxes with trappings of refuse to make it feel more like home. So long as we recognize our current situation for what it is, that it cannot provide the genuine article of fulfillment that we long for, we can endure. As we endure, we temper our hope with the expectation of Heaven as God works in tandem with us to manage our lives, desires, and disappointments. And, eventually, we will find our way Home together.

Scripture: *Clothe yourselves with the Lord Jesus Christ, and do not think about how to gratify the desires of the flesh. - Romans 13:14 NIV*

Thought: Greed is a self-defense mechanism we use to find fulfillment independently. When we use Greed we will become addicted if we are able to take what we want. The guilt inherent to addiction creates self-loathing, which makes us even more likely to return to our addictions. God calls us to return to Faith by accepting the garment of Christ, which frees us from sin and shame.

Questions:

- Which of your desires are you tempted to use Greed with?
- Why might you respond to others who are in Greed?
- How does the garment of Christ free us from Greed?

Chapter 5

APATHY

I denied myself nothing my eyes desired; I refused my heart no pleasure. My heart took delight in all my labor, and this was the reward for all my toil. Yet when I surveyed all that my hands had done and what I had toiled to achieve, everything was meaningless, a chasing after the wind; nothing was gained under the sun.

- Ecclesiastes 2:10-11 NIV

I am losing all hope; I am paralyzed with fear. I remember the days of old. I ponder all your great works and think about what you have done. I lift my hands to you in prayer. I thirst for you as parched land thirsts for rain. Come quickly, Lord, and answer me, for my depression deepens. Don't turn away from me, or I will die.

- Psalm 143:4-7 NLT

Longing for Perfection

I can't eat steak whenever I go out to eat. I won't order it. I don't have dietary restrictions. I've never had an adverse reaction to eating steak. Truth be told, I quite enjoy steak. Many of the steaks I have eaten I'm sure were quite good - objectively speaking. So, why can't I eat steak? The problem is that I grew up being accustomed to the best steak conceivably possible.

My dad grills steak the way that my grandfather taught him. I, myself, haven't yet even attempted to grill a steak like they do. When they cook steak they buy filet mignon - the smaller, higher quality portion of a steak tenderloin. Tenderloin is already considered to be the most tender cut of meat you can get from an animal, hence the name. So, in essence, this makes the filet mignon the best of the best, and quite expensive as a result. Filet mignon grilled to perfection, with time-tested methods passed down generation to generation, was a staple of a nice meal growing up.

As my wife says, it makes all other steaks "turn to ash in my mouth." Essentially, I've become a steak snob. Nothing comes close to my family's steak. Not by a long shot. On one occasion my dad and I went out to eat, ordered steak, and got a bite or two in before we decided to box it up, go home, and grill our own. Is it then fair to say that eating filet mignon ruined steak for me? It sure seems that way.

If I hadn't exclusively eaten filet mignon during my formative years, would I still feel the same way about restaurant steaks? Doubtfully. Without having home-grilled filet mignon to compare them to, I imagine that I would have enjoyed restaurant steaks just fine, probably far more than I currently do so. Ignorance is bliss, as they say. Because my taste buds have been routinely exposed to the best steak, "good" steak has become less enjoyable. This is an interesting conundrum - we long for perfection, but then perfection seems to spoil us. We might enjoy something well enough, but then as soon as we see or experience something better, what we have seems to lose its shine. But there's something more powerful, more core to who we are, that's at work here.

About a year ago, my son begged me for a toy truck he saw in a convenience store. I knew as soon as he saw it, we were in trouble. I had the awareness to prep him for our trip, explaining that we wouldn't get any toys on this trip out. Yet, despite my cautioning, this truck caught his eye. For better or worse, the only way I managed to make it out of the store with him in tow was to take a picture of his prized truck and promise that, if he behaved well, we could return to get it some other time. For days afterward he would bring it up, talking about how cool the truck was and how excited he was about it, before asking if we could go get it, of course. When I finally agreed to take him to go purchase it, you'd have thought I just told him we were going to Disney World. For about a week after buying it, it was all he wanted to play with. Fast forward to today, however, and it's no more special to him than any of his other toys.

We can all relate to this. We find something that we think will satisfy us completely, but then it disappoints or bores us. Call it entitlement, buyer's remorse, boredom, or whatever you'd like, but the issue is the same: our hearts refuse to be satisfied by this world. You could buy your dream home, your own little slice of Heaven all to yourself. But give it some time and you'll start longing for more.

What does it mean to you that even some of the best things in this world fail to fulfill you completely? What does that tell you about who you are? About what your heart is longing for? If this world were all we knew or all we were meant for, then surely we wouldn't feel the discontent we experience so rampantly. The longings we feel for perfection are meant to drive us to God and to Heaven - our true home. Everything else under the sun will fail us. In this reality, we have a choice: to spurn our discontent and come to hate the world for not being enough, or to allow our longings to point us towards what really matters. Our understanding of disappointment is in dire need of examining, lest we come to despise our very nature.

When we are disappointed something foul can happen in the human heart. Rather than grieving our disappointment and clinging to hope, we may give up hope and subsequently lose sight of our desires. Maintaining hope in the course of repeated disappointment can seem impossible, or at least unnecessarily painful. We become apathetic when we assume our problem is not that we are unable to have our desires fulfilled, but that we have any desires at all. This is the quadrant of Apathy, where disappointment has become such an apparent inevitability that we come to believe desire and hope only set us up to be disappointed and hurt. If hope and desire always end poorly, then Apathy believes it is only logical to give them up to resignation. Rather than accepting that disappointment helps us, Apathy gives up the hope that there's anything more.

Apathy is a form of self-protecting where we refuse to have hope or desire so as to avoid more pain or disappointment. Generally, Apathy is developed after repeated, failed attempts to find fulfillment. While it is possible to jump straight from Faith to Apathy, most will first linger in Manipulation or Greed. When those strategies inevitably fail us, we find ourselves creeping towards Apathy. We go from Manipulation to Apathy through the door of relational insecurity, which is the belief that no one can be trusted or counted upon, and so we try to kill our need for relationship. We go from Greed to Apathy through the door of futility - the belief that nothing we do will matter or make a difference, and so we attempt to numb ourselves to our unmet desires.

Essentially, Apathy can be thought of as simply giving up - not caring about your desires nor your relationships. It is a lack of care for yourself and others. Apathy gives up because it doesn't understand that disappointment has a purpose, that it is pruning us into the people we are meant to be. All Apathy sees is the discomfort, not the shape that we are being molded into. It believes that *nothing* will ever satisfy, and that desires and relationships are therefore naive and pain-inducing. It believes that Heaven is either a myth, or insists that "If I only had _____, then I would feel happy again," not realizing that happiness isn't obtained by reaching a goal, but instead by being on the pathway to *The* Goal. And yet, Apathy is not a conclusion that we easily arrive at. Something in us will rebel at giving up hope, even when our hope seems slim.

Most of us resist giving in to apathetic thinking. It doesn't come naturally. One might assume that Apathy comes about by significant disappointments or tragedies. But, while tragedies can certainly happen to us, plenty of people end up apathetic without a preceding crisis. Curiously, Apathy seems to occur most often as a result of small grievances - an accumulation of all the little inconveniences we try to ignore or don't take as seriously. Jean Webster[1] has a quote that captures the essence of this thought:

"It isn't the big troubles in life that require character. Anybody can rise to a crisis and face a crushing tragedy with courage, but to meet the petty hazards of the day with a laugh - I really think that requires spirit. It's the kind of character that I am going to develop."
- Jean Webster

This perspective is staggering. It deserves saying again: the courage to deal with a crisis is commonplace. Rather, it is rare to laugh about the "petty hazards of the day." We typically think courageous heroes are the ones who arise in time of great peril, not the ones who are able to shrug off an interruption. While I believe that bravely confronting a crisis *is* admirable, I agree with Webster - it is exceedingly rare for people to respond courageously to all the minor problems that drive us crazy. People typically overlook the minute problems until we cannot bear them any longer, then chastise ourselves for being unreasonably sad, angry, or stressed. All too easily the day's negativity saps our resolve because, although the petty hazards affect us, we don't heed them for the trouble they really are. I'm not saying that we have to cry over spilt milk, but that we learn to accept and manage reality. We cannot expect Earth to be Heaven. Because the truth is that life is full of these "petty hazards of the day."

The trash bag breaks on your way to the dumpster and spills garbage everywhere.

You realize the library books are a week overdue.

A friend didn't return your text.

The freezer stops working.

Your car's Check Engine light comes on.

An eyelash gets lodged in your eye.

And that can just be in the first few hours of the day. On and on it goes, the problems compounding upon one another until we reach a boiling point. If courage to face the petty hazards is scarce, then it follows that most of us respond to them inadequately. Perhaps we rant and rail about the problems, groaning and cursing when life doesn't seem to go our way. Maybe we try to ignore the problems. We may seek momentary comfort through the means of Greed, or try to force life to work the way we want through Manipulation.

While Greed and Manipulation may cause a mess, they are different from Apathy because they still maintain hope that they can still somehow find fulfillment. Greed and Manipulation try to make life suit our whims but they are ineffective. Eventually, given enough time and circumstance, both Greed and Manipulation leave us disappointed. Then Apathy grows within our hearts as we are constantly assaulted by the troubles of life. Finally, rather than learning how to manage our desires, we give up the hope that our desires matter. The loss of desire manifests like an infection, beginning with the original disappointment and spreading until it dominates our entire being.

Apathy doesn't seek to change things externally, but internally. In this, Apathy nearly hits the mark; ultimately we cannot force the world to conform to our whims. We indeed need to have a look at ourselves and our choices. But the part that Apathy gets wrong is vital. Rather than meeting the troubles of life one way or another, Apathy attempts to remove our beating heart to cope with the pain. It eliminates any semblances of desire, because it believes that desires only bring suffering. The words of Christ challenge this thinking:

On the last and greatest day of the festival, Jesus stood and said in a loud voice, "Let anyone who is thirsty come to me and drink. Whoever believes in me, as Scripture has said, rivers of living water will flow from within them."
- John 7:37-38 NIV

Obviously, Jesus is not talking about literal thirst. He's not at the synagogue handing out cups of water. So what is he talking about? Jesus is equating the carnal desire of thirst to the soul-deep longing for perfection, life, and eternity. He is inviting those who aren't satisfied with this life to come to him.

"Whoever eats my flesh and drinks my blood has eternal life, and I will raise them up at the last day. (…) Just as the living Father sent me and I live because of the Father, so the one who feeds on me will live because of me."
- John 6:54;57 NIV

It's as if he is saying, "Not satisfied with those T-bone steaks? I can give you the filet mignon of your dreams! But here's the secret - I'm the filet. I am what you've been looking for." Disappointment, which Apathy tries to avoid at all cost, is not the enemy. It is one of the driving forces that leads us to our savior. If we have killed our desires, if we are no longer "thirsty," then we will not come to Christ to drink.

Picture two thirsty people taking opposing approaches. One looks everywhere for water, while the other one sits hopelessly, resigned to death by dehydration. Although the former may get into some trouble in his frantic search for water, his desire may eventually lead him to water. The latter looks more "civilized" in his unobtrusiveness, but he has consigned himself to death by forfeiting even an acknowledgement of his thirst. Even if someone were to offer him a cup of water, it is nearly impossible to get him to accept it. He declines because he believes it is "too late," or that nothing can satisfy him. Similarly, if we resolve to bury our desires and accept Apathy, we will inhibit our relationship with Christ. On the other hand, Jesus accepts the sinner who turns to him, despite the mess that might have been created in the sinner's frantic search for fulfillment.

It's easy to know when we're operating in Manipulation or Greed. They leave a wake of chaos in their path, trying desperately to get their desires met. But Apathy can be notoriously difficult to spot. The very purpose of Apathy is to avoid drawing attention to hope and desire, so it also avoids the others' attention. Those living in Apathy will try to get you to look away. Think the stereotypical, sullen teenager. The kid who only answers, "good," "nothing," or "I don't know," to every question asked of them:

"How was your day?"

"Good."

"What did you do?"

"Nothing."

Indeed, such a conversation is "good for nothing." This may come as a surprise, but few Apathetic people will complain about their circumstances. I say this because many people seem to confuse opposition with depression. Apathetic people will not make their opinion known, whether good or bad. Apathy doesn't look like unhappiness or resistance, it looks like someone who doesn't care one way or the other. In other words, when we say "no," to something, we are likely saying "yes," to something else:

"Do you want to watch a movie?"

"No, I'd rather watch a TV show."

That isn't Apathy, it's healthy communication. The obvious exception is when someone says "no" to seemingly every invitation, then doesn't know what they really want if they are pressed further. The point I'm making is that you cannot assume someone is Apathetic because they oppose you. Opposition doesn't feel nice, but at least we know *something* about what the person wants or doesn't want. Apathy, on the other hand, refuses to see any value, pain, or pleasure in anything. It is nihilistic, believing that nothing really matters and, therefore, nothing is all you get from them. Their words are only noise meant to keep you from engaging their resigned heart.

When asked to watch a movie, they might answer: "Okay," "No thanks," "Whatever you'd like to do," or "I don't care." Their Apathy isn't revealed in their responses, but in their overall disposition. They will say anything to keep you from looking too closely, even if that means agreeing with you. And if you manage to catch a hint of their Apathy and question them on what's wrong, you'll likely be told that it's either nothing or that you're being too nosy. Anything to keep you from engaging their lack of hope and desire, because they believe there's no point to it. In their estimation, it's already "too late."

We try to hide behind Apathy, refusing to be seen with our individual wants and needs, likes and dislikes. Apathy would rather have us blend in and compromise our individuality for the sake of conflict avoidance. Anything to avoid pain. Apathy compels us to denial - acting as though nothing were wrong. But avoidance won't get us far. Addressing life's problems requires more, because the world remains a jagged place even if we pretend it is not.

"In this world you will have trouble…"
- John 16:33b NIV

Jesus guarantees us that we will encounter trouble one way or another. If you imagine that you can make the troubles of life go away by pretending not to be bothered, then you are setting yourself up for failure. We ought to know by now that the world is not a safe place. Yet, there is still a part of us that wants the world to be comfortable, even if that comfort is gained by denying the trouble that bothers us. It doesn't work - we cannot decide to not be bothered. All we *can* do is learn how to channel our botherdness so that we learn to appreciate it, not fight it. The desire for goodness (and, therefore, our abhorrence for trouble) comes from the core of our being - from the heart that was meant for perfect intimacy and longs for restoration in eternity:

Yet God has made everything beautiful for its own time. He has planted eternity in the human heart…

- Ecclesiastes 3:11a NLT

We long for our home. Everything God-given longing we have points us that way. To Eden. To Heaven. To God. In fact, we are so inclined for perfection that goodness becomes taken for granted once we've grown accustomed to it. We are far more bothered by inconvenience than we are grateful for convenience.

We are juxtaposed: our inner being longs to live in perfection, but our reality in this life is constant trouble. At first glance, Apathy seems like a good remedy to this conundrum. If we could simply mitigate the difficulties by choosing to not be bothered, there'd be no issue. If you didn't want to hurt, then you wouldn't. But it doesn't take a genius to know that's not possible. Despite what some might believe, we can never truly get used to pain and discomfort. Pretending to be "fine" is not the same thing as truly thriving. We have to deal with the painful reality in a productive way. As it is, Apathy tries to deal with reality by having an unrealistic goal. It is a self-defeating process: Apathy causes us to anticipate disappointment to avoid disappointment.

Apathy exchanges desires of every shape and color for the sole desire of avoiding pain, and thus is an ill-suited stance to engage life, since pain is a given. Apathy erroneously believes that one can escape the trouble of the fallen world, even if it so happens to be through killing the hopeful parts of ourselves. As if killing a part of your own heart weren't problematic enough, the inescapable truth is that trouble will meet you wherever you go in this life, in whatever state you are in. Apathy thinks that it can avoid pain, such as the pain of disappointment, by ridding itself of hope. But the problem is that trouble and pain don't discriminate between optimists and pessimists. Life is relentless in its sweetness and bitterness, regardless of whether or not we hope or despair. The only thing we can ultimately change is our own disposition. And so the work to avoid pain by ridding ourselves of hope is futile. It doesn't stave off hardship, only guarantees that we will miss life's treasured delights. Apathy, in an attempt to seal off the heart off from further pain, also closes the heart's eyes to beauty, goodness, and delight.

If we try to stop ourselves from being disappointed, we are inherently attempting to kill our own hearts, which are meant for eternity. Acceptance is not complacently settling for less (as Apathy would have you think), it is the acceptance that we were meant for more and live in a place that offers less. The part of you that desires permanent goodness and aches at the petty hazards will endure forever. Thus, Apathy is ultimately an attempt to numb ourselves to the part of ourselves that cannot be destroyed. We are meant to ache for God to set things right.

He will wipe every tear from their eyes. There will be no more death or mourning or crying or pain, for the old order of things has passed away.
- Revelation 21:4 NIV

God promises us a blissful new existence where pain and disappointment are done away with. *That* is what we are longing for. No more tears. No more pain. This new existence is accomplished by "the old order of things" being expired, *not* by God changing our ability to endure disappointment. Said differently, God will change the world to suit our hearts, not our hearts to suit the world. Your eternal soul, which cannot be done away with and is an alien to this strange world, longs for the coming perfection. Trying to change ourselves to suit our current environment, then, is foolishness. We're in line for it, and must find a way to accept that.

Thus, trouble multiplies from the sisyphean effort Apathy puts into performing an impossible task - we try to stop ourselves from being disappointed (which is the same as saying we try to stop longing for God/Heaven/The new order). But we are unable to do so. In fact, the effort backfires. When we try to stop hurting, we wind up being unable to enjoy any goodness at all.

The Black Hole

When we suffer, our ability to enjoy goodness is threatened. Pain tempts us to tune out the world in its entirety. If the world were only a bleak and unforgiving hell, this wouldn't be a problem. But the world, with all its troubles and delights, keeps right on spinning despite however horrific or menial our troubles may be. Goodness is just as relentless as badness. In the midst of our pain there will be crimson sunrises and sunsets, newborn babies, the first verdant budding of spring, the amber vibrancy of autumn, towering mountains, thundering waterfalls, or perhaps some kind words from a friend. Beauty abounds in creation despite the horror that seeks to mar it. David writes:

The heavens declare the glory of God; the skies proclaim the work of his hands.

- Psalm 19:1 NIV

It is easy to miss the proclamation of the skies when our hearts are burdened with suffering.

A few years ago I attended a conference in Colorado, and I made a point to rent a Jeep and drive along the winding highways following the Rockies. It was my first visit to Colorado - something I had dreamed of doing for years. I felt the allure of the looming mountains as they dominated the western horizon. A couple of days later, my midwestern eyes took in a sight I had never seen before: the sun slowly descending behind the Rocky Mountains. The scene looked like something I had only ever seen in paintings. I admired the view for a second before I thought to take out my phone, stand on my Jeep's rear bumper, and take a picture of the sunset. Then I jumped down and drove off to my hotel.

That night, following a prompting we received at the conference, I prayed to experience the goodness and delight of God. It wasn't long before I had the sense that God had already tried to give me exactly what I had asked for. His goodness, majesty, and care was offered to me in that sunset. Immediately, I longed to return to that moment and linger far longer. I imagined myself climbing onto the roof of my Jeep and watching the sunset until the stars came out. Not simply taking a picture like a tourist and moving on. I missed that opportunity, and I was determined not to miss the next one.

I can't help but wonder... How many moments like this do we miss on a regular basis? Moments where God wants to impart some goodness to us. If we can miss beauty even when we are looking for it, how much more are we oblivious if we're preoccupied? The truth is unsettling: we seem to numb ourselves to the very things we long for. We want a vacation, but then experience it indifferently. Similarly, we try to restrict God to doing only what we want him to do and miss out on what he *is* doing. We are blinded by busyness, our preoccupations, and narrow-mindedness. God is an extravagant lover, more so than we can palate. If we take scripture at its word, that *every* good gift is from God himself, then we indeed miss out on much of the goodness being given to us.

There was a story I heard a number of years ago. I cannot recall where I heard it from. I'm not even sure if it's true, but it reveals a powerful truth. A man received a corrective surgery for his vision, allowing him to see clearly for the first time in his life. His friends took him on a scenic drive along the northern coast of California. After hours of driving, they were dismayed when they saw that he wasn't even looking out the window. When they asked him what he was looking at, he explained that he was absolutely captivated by the motes of dust inside the car, glowing softly in the light of a sunbeam. Sunsets, rocks, horizons, and beaches had been explained to him, he said. But no one had ever told him about the beauty of dust catching sunlight passing through a window.

There is rich beauty all around us. It's so commonplace that we often fail to recognize it at all. Even worse, in the midst of Apathy, we may notice goodness, but reject it out of suspicion or curse it bitterly. Because how dare there be beauty when we are suffering?! Despite our hard-heartedness, God and the beauty of his creation remain available. That beauty is as common as motes of dust. If we're looking to find it, we need only ask and look. But Apathy isn't searching for goodness or beauty. It considers such things to be a trap, setting us up for only more pain. Apathy causes us to anticipate disappointment in an effort to avoid the inevitable letdowns that life carries with it. As a result, when good things happen to Apathetic people, they are unable to enjoy it. They are too preoccupied by looking for something bad to happen. So they discredit goodness by rejecting it outright and instead focus only on the real or imagined negativity they anticipate. Apathy refuses to enjoy goodness or delight because it associates hope with the pain of disappointment - no exceptions. When we reach this point, even some of the best things in this world will fail to elicit even a hint of joy:

"Hey, I heard your family got a new puppy! Are you excited?"
"Nah, I'm not letting myself get attached. It'll die someday."

"How was your vacation to the Bahamas?"
"What does it matter? It's over now."

The problem with Apathy is that, in part, it isn't wrong. Apathy doesn't trust anything good because it knows that goodness in this world is temporary. Which is true. However, while Earth goodness is not permanent, it points to a coming goodness that will be. Transient goodness hurts us because we have an innate longing for eternal goodness and everlasting peace. If we don't have a realistic hope in eternal goodness, then our desires only bring futility. In other words, Apathy is guilty of confirmation bias - it filters out the positive to fit a pre-existing theory that everything is negative.

We live in a broken, fallen world where there is always trouble. If you look for something to be disappointed about, you'll find it. The puppy *will* eventually die, the vacation *will* come to an end. Most scientists agree that the sun will eventually expand into a red giant, destroying the Earth and consuming all of the inner planets. But life will have probably been obliterated from the Earth far before then due to the oceans boiling away from the sun's increased heat. On this side of eternity, all beauty has an expiration date. Destruction seems inevitable in our own lives just as much as the apparent fate of the Earth. So what can we do about the awful inevitability we find to be true? Do we simply give way to resignation, set our minds on refusing the negative outcome, or something else?

Apathy despises the incongruence between our longings and our apparent reality, and also believes that the negative reality cannot be changed. So rather than trying to change reality it seeks to kill our longings - to acquiesce to hopelessness. Therefore, anything that stirs the heart to hope is treated as naive foolishness.

I do not mean to imply that we have to force ourselves to enjoy things when we are hurting, only that as true goodness comes our way, we turn towards it. When I feel sad, I do not enjoy watching comedy. It doesn't seem appropriate at the time, but that doesn't mean that all goodness is. Going for a walk along a creekside or looking at the stars proves to do the trick. Discerning what goodness is available to us and allowing ourselves the room to receive it matters. Goodness helps us to heal and to enjoy life as we look forward with hope. But Apathy rejects all kinds of goodness and beauty, and locks itself away with its miseries. It causes us to be offended that others might possibly enjoy beauty and goodness while we suffer.

Apathy does not and cannot have faith in goodness; the only faith it has is in the inevitability of pain. So pain is all Apathy grants us. Sadly, perpetual pain is the self-fulfilling prophecy created by Apathy. Since Apathy believes that desires will only bring about pain, it avoids, kills, or sabotages desire. Since it defines existence by the avoidance of pain rather than the pursuit of desire, all it can measure life by is pain. Even if something good were to happen, Apathy cannot be pleased, yet cannot be proven wrong. When something goes right it only sees a trap and anticipates the inevitable return of disappointment and suffering.

The thing that Apathy fails to understand is that it is not the things themselves (whether comedy, creeks, stars, or anything else) that are helpful, but the care of God received through them. While the vessels of God's affection may come and go, they are meant to point us towards the eternal giver - our God in whom the fulfillment of all we long for might be found. The temporary goodness of this world, like any decent appetizer, is neither meant to be our source of fulfillment nor discouragement. Goodness is meant to draw our hearts to ache for the fulfillment of God's promises. Yet if Apathy treats goodness with such derision, what happens when trouble happens to Apathetic people?

Every good thing in the world, as it currently is, will come to an end. From ashes, to ashes, as scripture says. Apathy tries to anticipate disappointment to avoid the pain of disappointment, but this tactic fails. When goodness is present, it is rejected under suspicion for only causing more inevitable pain when it fails. So, when those stuck in an Apathetic mindset encounter the disappointment they were anticipating, they take it as proof that they were right to be pessimistic. Disappointment reinforces Apathy, fueling it with more "evidence" that goodness fails and suffering lasts.

Goodness grants us only brief glimpses of life as we know it was meant to be. Perfect, permanent, enrapturing goodness. The resilient, faithful soul that hopes in God takes this life as an appetizer and grows in anticipation for God's main course. But Apathy hates that the appetizer doesn't fulfill. It feeds on life like a black hole, sucking out even the tiniest morsel of joy by only observing how disappointing the appetizer is. All of the "evidence" that Apathy takes to rationalize itself will only snowball until it becomes depression. Inevitably, Apathy causes us to lose pleasure in everything. The more "evidence" Apathy collects, the more crushed we become by it.

As astrophysicists will sometimes say, black holes are actually rather simple objects. They might wreak havoc on everything around them, distorting spacetime into a nauseating mess, but the actual object that causes it is rather simple. Similarly, Apathy isn't very complicated, but it weaves a trap that can feel impossible to escape.

Escape

Recovering from Apathy is particularly difficult because Apathy causes us to lose the hope that things can get better. The desire to change Apathy *is* the battle of Apathy. Apathy perceives disappointment so rampantly, it believes that nothing can be done. Hope becomes futile.

Repeatedly in scripture, God equates the loss of hope to death:

Then he said to me: "Son of man, these bones are the people of Israel. They say, 'Our bones are dried up and our hope is gone; we are cut off.' Therefore prophesy and say to them: 'This is what the Sovereign Lord says: My people, I am going to open your graves and bring you up from them; I will bring you back to the land of Israel."

- Ezekiel 37:11 NIV

We do not want you to be uninformed, brothers and sisters, about the troubles we experienced in the province of Asia. We were under great pressure, far beyond our ability to endure, so that we despaired of life itself. Indeed, we felt we had received the sentence of death.

- 2 Corinthians 1:8-9a NIV

Imagine that you receive a terminal diagnosis: you have 6 months left to live. There is no cure, nor treatment. You can be made comfortable, but it is inevitable. You will die. You now face a terrible choice: refuse to accept the truth and spend your remaining time frantically looking for a miracle cure (Which can be considered Manipulation or Greed), completely give up and resign yourself to waiting for death (Apathy), or to make the most of the time that you have left (Faith). To give into Apathy is to die long before you are truly dead. Indeed, many who struggle with depression and hopelessness feel like they are already gone.

Losing the hope that things can get better can make the rest of life appear pointless. If we do not have hope, then what good are our desires? In other words, if I believed that filet mignon were only a figment of my imagination, then my desire for better steak would be a living nightmare. Nothing would satisfy. The only course of action would be to eliminate my desire and hope because I cannot foresee any possible positive outcome. Losing our hope and desire makes the end seem like it's already been written. In order to escape Apathy, we have to relearn how to have hope, even in the face of inevitable disappointment. Towards this end, we are aided by our disappointments, for they reveal that our hearts are not truly content with misery. The problem is not our pain, it's what we do with our pain.

Our hearts - the core, eternal soul that you are - will go on longing even if you tell it not to. Giving up hope is impossible; for giving up hope is only done *in the hope* that losing hope will stymie our pain. Our hearts are made to yearn for perfect love, and cannot, *will* not, be stopped. Apathy tries to escape that reality - that pain. Numbing ourselves to our insatiable desires for goodness might seem to work for a time. But if our disposition is to avoid pain, when our hope starts to spring back up, we will move against it. It is a conundrum: to truly manage discomfort, we must appreciate discomfort rather than despise it.

This is not a call to reckless self-infliction or machismo. Nothing is gained by neither inflicting harm on yourself nor needlessly enduring suffering that can easily be treated. The point is about learning to embrace our pain; to push through adversity and the way it causes us to live in fear. Apathy wants the hurt to go away entirely, and shirks away from discomfort. But the truth of the matter is that our pain, and our aversion to pain, teach us important lessons. Acting like we're not hurting gets us nowhere and only perpetuates an unhelpful belief that to feel pain, disappointment, sadness, worry, and hopelessness is a sign of weakness. It is not. Disappointment, trouble, and hardship can only exist when they are contrasted to the goodness that we know we are meant for.

In order to know what is bad, we must also know what is good. So, although an embittered soul might appear resigned to melancholy, it is only because they cannot stop their heart from aching for God. The trouble of this world is similar to the difference between light and darkness - darkness is not a "thing," it is only the absence of the light. If the earth were perpetually shrouded in darkness, we would only complain about the dark if we somehow knew there was such a thing as light. Otherwise we would simply accept the darkness as normal. So the fact that our hearts complain about life's troubles must mean that our hearts know something better exists. Suffering is only "bad" because it in some way thwarts what we know to be "good."

Our hearts are meant for hope that cannot be revoked. When we feel disappointed, it is not a sign that something is wrong with us. Disappointment is a sign that we aren't home yet. Regret is not the final word that we are failures, only that we are becoming the people that God meant us to be. As such, perseverance is not best defined as our ability to endure disappointment, but as the wisdom to manage our eternity-aching hearts well. Without the need we innately have for Heaven and for God, pain wouldn't bother us. That is why it is so problematic that Apathy anticipates disappointment - it tries to solely endure hardships without dealing with the root cause of disappointment.

Apathy fails to examine what lessons pain can teach us. In other words, our flaws and failures can show us what we can improve - not because we must (for we are covered by grace), but because we desire to. Maya Angelou once wrote,

"Do the best you can until you know better. Then when you know better, do better."

Our pain, disappointment, and failures are not meant to be avoided, but to teach us about who are, and who we're meant to be. Disappointment is a symptom of a heart that knows it was meant for more. And, for the time being, the good that we can focus our energy on is not a guaranteed positive outcome, but rather on doing the best we can. We must look ahead to what we can do better, rather than chastising our past selves for not knowing better. But, in order to do so, it is critical that we pay attention to how we respond to setbacks.

It is a death sentence to merely take on the hardships of life without examining how we are weathering them. Our hearts require constant upkeep. Like a ship on rough seas, we need at least occasional reprieve to assess the damage and make repairs. If we do not appreciate and care for the aching of our hearts, we will come to despise the nagging pain we bear. When Apathy prompts us to start anticipating and looking for disappointment, it is an attempt to change a heart that was designed to anticipate goodness.

> *Hope deferred makes the heart sick, but a longing fulfilled is a tree of life.*
> *- Proverbs 13:12 NIV*

If hope deferred makes the heart sick, then having no hope at all is an attempt to kill the heart. Goodness no longer matters to us when we give up hope. We've locked away the deep longings of our heart and thrown away the keys. Thus, we are confined to an existence where we are alienated from ourselves. In this way, we become our own worst enemy. We damn ourselves to an existence where our fear has striped us of any pleasure.

But our hearts still go right on aching. In our attempt to be rid ourselves of pain, all we end up losing is our delight. We want that "tree of life," but Apathy causes us to be unable to endure the longing that precedes it. So all we're left with is hope deferred and a sick heart. Good thing we have a God who raises the dead.

To change our Apathy, we must become "sick and tired of being sick and tired." We have to begin hoping that things can get better, and be willing to endure longing once again.

There's good news.

If you decide and commit to trying your hardest, you've already succeeded. We do not have to expend our effort trying to make life all good or all bad. All we have to do is look at what is within our control, then do our best. Success isn't about guaranteeing positive outcomes, it is about knowing you've done everything you can do. The old, black and white kind of thinking doesn't do us much good. It causes us to view life with either sheer optimism or pessimism. The optimist denies the existence of any negativity and life, and is setting themselves up for a rude awakening. The pessimist denies all the positives of life, and lives in resignation. We need a worldview that allows us to manage the hardships of life between the extremes of denial and resignation.

Acknowledgement is a good place to start, I think. Acknowledgement is being able to name things as they are, while being as objective as possible. It doesn't mean that we accept things the way they are without doing anything about it. It does mean that we look within ourselves and begin to survey what is happening, and how we are responding. Doing so, we no longer define ourselves by mere external circumstances, but also the quality of our internal responses. This process frees us from reactionary behavior, which is driven by impulses that oftentimes make matters worse. Instead, acknowledgement helps us to be informed by our feelings, rather than ruled by them.

If there is one thing that Apathy must acknowledge, it is the reality that disappointment is indeed inevitable, but that doesn't mean there isn't also some goodness. In the deepest, darkest pit of Apathy lies a springboard: if disappointment cannot be stopped, then what do we have to lose by hoping? As the saying goes, it is better to have tried and failed than to have never tried at all. The pain of hopelessness is worse than that of disappointment. What's more, when we define success not by what we achieve, but instead by a measure of our own effort, then success is entirely within our control. Nothing can stop us from trying, except ourselves. It is a greater test of character to continually try your best than to "succeed" at any given task.

So, what exactly are we trying to do? How should we expend our effort? We are trying to cling to hope, and allow that hope to move us to action. We need a hope that no disappointment, not even death, can extinguish. It is not enough to hope that we're getting it right and won't mess up. We must hope that we can overcome whatever adversity lies ahead of us. That adversity is not primarily found in negative outcomes such as a terminal illness, but rather in the looming dread that causes us to give up prematurely. Fear is the enemy, not failure.

Remember the story of when Jesus walked on water? When the disciples see Jesus, they are initially terrified:

But Jesus immediately said to them: "Take courage! It is I. Don't be afraid."
"Lord, if it's you," Peter replied, "tell me to come to you on the water."

111

"Come," he said.

Then Peter got down out of the boat, walked on the water and came toward Jesus. But when he saw the wind, he was afraid and, beginning to sink, cried out, "Lord, save me!"

- Matthew 14:27-30 NIV

Peter's focus slipped. The problems that we face have a similar tendency. If we fix our gaze on Jesus, the one who overcame death, we find ourselves unburdened by the concerns that we would otherwise drown in. When Jesus plucks Peter from the water, He says:

"You of little faith," he said, "why did you doubt?"

- Matthew 14:31b NIV

This is just my personal opinion, but I think that Peter's doubt wasn't that he started questioning Jesus' divinity. After all, the man can still see Jesus standing on the water and calls out for Jesus to save him. No, I believe Peter's doubt is something that we are all familiar with: What if? Remember, Peter was a fisherman, and undoubtedly well acquainted with the dangers of water. "That wind seems really strong, and those waves are getting really big. What if they knock me over?" I wonder if Peter's heart started pounding. Did his vision tunnel and his palms begin to sweat? Did he wonder, "What if I drown?" Those thoughts and feelings are surely only made worse when the water starts rising past his ankles. The fear of the wind and waves wins out over the desire to be with Christ. It bears saying again: The *possibility* of trouble conquers the *certainty* of Christ.

As soon as fear takes hold and begins to drive our behavior, it will always sap our desire and cause our efforts to waver. But why do our efforts matter so much? It's simple. The secret to effort is Faith. We will only take action when we have a fundamental belief that our actions matter; even if our actions cannot influence the outcome. Hence why the Bible asserts that faith without works is dead! Our hope in Christ is revealed by our ability to try, even when "failure" seems certain. In fact, trouble is always certain:

"I have told you these things, so that in me you may have peace. In this world you will have trouble. But take heart! I have overcome the world."
- John 16:33 NIV

We are commanded to take heart, not take victory. We don't have to concern ourselves with achieving positive results, as the victory has already been won by Christ. Our goal is to be encouraged and live like we've already won, even in the face of adversity. Jesus does not promise to make our lives easier. He promises that it will be hard. Instead of a free pass, he gives us himself and his victory. In him we see God's promise, the hope all other hopes hinge upon:

He will wipe every tear from their eyes. There will be no more death or mourning or crying or pain, for the old order of things has passed away.
- Revelation 21:4 NIV

Rather than disappointment fueling even more Apathy, through faith in Christ trouble and hardship become the continual reminders that something better is coming - something that our hearts desperately long for. We see that tribulations, rather than bringing us only pain, bring us closer to Christ. With this newfound confidence, we no longer fear hardship. Being rid of that fear nips Apathy in the bud. Instead of causing fear, trouble is seen as the passing reality, not the permanent one. In the meantime, we can appreciate this world's goodness without living in anxiety that trouble will come and take it away.

In this life we know that pain and hardship will come. That does not mean we need to live in fear of it. As surely as trouble comes, God promises that trouble has its days numbered. Jesus gives us every reason to hope, and that hope flips everything on Apathy's head. Trusting Christ enables us to enjoy this world as it is and appreciate the disappointments as only whetting our appetite for the permanent goodness that is to come:

When a woman is giving birth, she has sorrow because her hour has come, but when she has delivered the baby, she no longer remembers the anguish, for joy that a human being has been born into the world.

So also you have sorrow now, but I will see you again, and your hearts will rejoice, and no one will take your joy from you.

- John 16:21-22 ESV

Our ability to enjoy the momentary blessings of this life is derived from our hope of everlasting life. When we rest in the hope of salvation, we are able to participate with the beauty and goodness around us rather than cursing it for being ephemeral. When we lose that hope, we will interpret difficulties differently. Apathy makes us desperate, so that we cling to our handfuls of sand, not realizing that we are headed for life on an endless beach. The hope Christ offers, that of *everlasting* goodness, frees us from trying to make earthly delights into heavenly delights. In Christ's hope we greet earthly goodness as an appetizer of Heaven and understand that when the moment is over, the disappointment is only a reminder that there will come a day when goodness and beauty will not end.

Scripture: *May the God of hope fill you with all joy and peace as you trust in him, so that you may overflow with hope by the power of the Holy Spirit. - Romans 15:13 NIV*

Thought: Apathy, the death of desire and hope, is a pervasive condition that we are unable to correct on our own. Jesus frees us from Apathy by offering himself to us - the only one to overcome the world and conquer death.

Questions:

- What has caused you to lose hope?
- Have you ever dealt with someone caught in Apathy? What was it like for you? For them?
- How might you share the gospel with someone stuck living in Apathy?

Chapter 6

COURAGEOUS VULNERABILITY

"Be still, and know that I am God;
I will be exalted among the nations,
I will be exalted in the earth."
- Psalm 46:10 NIV

Lord my God, I called to you for help,
and you healed me.
- Psalm 30:2 NIV

Courage

There are numerous scenes from the movie, *How to Train Your Dragon*[1], that embody the notion of Faith remarkably well. The protagonist, eager to bond with a ferocious dragon yet also terrified of being eaten alive, makes a bold move. He holds his hand up before the dragon, palm extended, and looks away. The dragon now has the power. It could flee or attack at any moment. But, after a careful sniff, the dragon gently presses his muzzle onto the boy's palm. They have made a connection, and they each lower their guards.

Such vulnerability takes tremendous courage. It is, tragically, all too often mistaken for cowardice or weakness. But cowards do not live in their vulnerability. They will either flee or feign toughness to hide their vulnerability. It takes real grit to neither run away nor force your way.

Anyone can pretend to be strong, and running away is easy. But it takes true strength to show vulnerability.

In the moment, it typically doesn't feel empowering to be vulnerable. In fact, it's terrifying. But at the end of the day, the choices we made to be vulnerable and courageous are the ones that matter. Vulnerability and Faith go hand in hand. They each require the other. To live a life of Faith we must be willing to be vulnerable, to be our authentic selves. But what goal, what destination, drives us to take such a risk?

We've spent four chapters discussing the various ways of handling our desires and relationships with the quadrants of Faith, Manipulation, Greed, and Apathy. We've concluded that what matters is not whether or not we have our desires fulfilled, but in how we seek out gratification. When we choose to handle our desires and our relationships with Faith, it opens the door to fulfillment. Real fulfillment. No other option will get you there, not by a long shot. Even when we obtain what we thought we most desired, if it is not obtained through Faith, it will leave us disappointed. Gratification obtained through Manipulation makes us anxious, Greed makes us addicted, and Apathy leaves us bitter and hopeless.

Clearly, Faith is the best option. But there's a catch. Mere knowledge that the quadrant of Faith is the only productive path is insufficient to motivate us to actually put it into practice. Knowledge is not enough to get us past the vulnerability that Faith requires. We need a conviction to drive our behavior, and this conviction must be greater than ourselves. A selfish goal will not suffer selfless tribulations. To live in Faith, we must be changed from the inside-out.

In grad school, I learned that trying to change people's behavior is ridiculously difficult. A hypothetical example I heard went something like this: A person is on the verge of heart disease due to their poor diet and exercise. Their doctor gives them a serious warning: if they do not change their habits, they will die prematurely. But, after they are warned by their doctor, they refuse to change their eating or exercise habits. They choose a familiar death over an unfamiliar change that will save their life. In the same way, we become accustomed to handling our desires and relationships in whatever fashion we have been, and we oftentimes stay there even when we recognize it isn't working. We tell ourselves that it's too late or too difficult to change. Losing our sense of control, which causes us to feel vulnerable, seems too difficult a task even if we know it will save our lives.

A few years ago, I counseled a husband and wife on the brink of divorce. It was neither spouse's first marriage, and they wanted help to save their new marriage. Watching them interact was painful - not because they argued, but because they acted so coldly towards one another. When I suggested and modeled what it might be like for them to talk more respectfully towards one another, I finally got them to agree on something. They both mocked what healthy communication sounds like: "Can you imagine us saying something like *that*?! 'I'm *sorry*, babe. Can you forgive me?' Ha! Are you serious?! Give me a break. Can you believe this guy?"

Sometimes the right course of action seems wrong to us when we've lived a certain way for too long. There is discomfort inherent to change, and we automatically assume discomfort means "wrong." If we don't recognize, accept, and plan for the discomfort inherent to change then we will be unable to choose better courses of action, even if we want to. I love this quote from one of my favorite authors, that so well depicts the difficulty of change:

"A journey will have pain and failure. It is not only the steps forward that we must accept. It is the stumbles. The trials. The knowledge that we will fail. That we will hurt those around us.

But if we stop, if we accept the person we are when we fail, the journey ends. That failure becomes our destination."

- Brandon Sanderson[2], Oathbringer

We will not grow simply because we know what to do or have been told what to do. We need more than information if we are to change the way we live. Growth is difficult, and our automatic tendency to avoid difficulty keeps us complacent. Having a motivating goal, one that is so important to us that we accept the difficulties inherent to change, is imperative.

I know of only one such goal: love. How would your life be changed if you lived in a constant state of truly feeling God's love? And how different is that than the daily life you live? God wants to romance us, not dull us to sleep. But first, God has to wake us out of our stupor and get us over our aversion to discomfort that keeps us from being authentically vulnerable.

So how does God shake us up, exactly? He astounds with wonder. He frustrates our logic. In essence, he uses beauty and pain.

A word of caution as we consider the concepts of beauty and pain; I do not want you to read "beauty and pain," as equivalent to "good and evil." Both beauty and pain are capable of being either good or bad. Remember, Satan disguised himself as a luminous angel (2 Corinthians 11:14) and God disciplines the children he loves (Proverbs 3:12). Beauty can be deceiving. Pain can be instructive. God uses both astounding goodness and humbling frustration to bring us back to our senses, and most of all, back to a vibrant relationship with him. While life with God undeniably grants us peace, it is nonetheless a wild goose chase. And thank God for that! A lifeless faith does little to stir the wild, human heart.

There is beauty when God grants us the desires of our heart, and pain when our desires are thwarted. Our desires, how they are met and how they are frustrated, are major components that affect our relationship with God. If the only thing driving us to live in Faith is to get what we want, disappointment will change our minds in a heartbeat.

Vulnerability requires that we recognize and give space for disappointment. If we insist on getting our way all the time, we will only run into resistance and pain. Our desire must not be for mere gratification, but for intimacy with the living God. It is this superior desire, the desire for a genuine relationship with God himself, that is the sole source of unfailing fulfillment. Real, authentic relationships require compromises. They are messy. Some conflict is inevitable. Working to avoid conflict has its merits, but it is far greater to concern yourself with preparing for when conflict happens. We must be ready to maintain our relationship with God when he doesn't do as we desire.

Real vulnerability and Faith have the capacity to endure disappointment when things don't go according to our expectations. However, the courage to endure becomes more difficult as we encounter repeated disappointments. Pain and rejection seem to teach us to guard ourselves rather than to become more vulnerable. Our instincts tell us to hide, run, and blame when we're hurt. We harbor fear of further injury, and express it as anger. It takes a lot to work past our anger and uncover the fear, and it's even harder to make the choice to trust and hope again afterwards. But when we do so, it shows our inner resolve and reveals that we are driven by a goal that's worth the risk.

It is one of the most genuine expressions of vulnerability, trust, and Faith when we choose to open ourselves back up again after we're hurt. It is someone who opens up to you and calmly tells you that you hurt their feelings. It is a child who seeks to understand why you disciplined them for being disobedient. It is a parent that apologizes after making a mistake. A young woman or man who goes back out on another first date after a bad breakup.

Our truest desires and beliefs are revealed in our response to adversity. It is easy to trust others when things always go according to plan. But once things become difficult we discover whether we really want intimacy (with all its pain and beauty), or if we just want control. Moments of courageous vulnerability show that we can look past our hurt to the *meaning* of the hurt. Understanding the inner turmoil we feel when we are disappointed enables us to know and pursue our dreams with more wisdom and freedom in the future. Vulnerability transforms us into humble self-advocates and keeps us from the counterfeits of resignation and control.

In choosing to be courageously vulnerable, we become willing to linger in unmet desires with Faith. This reveals that we fundamentally believe and hope in God's goodness despite our momentary discomfort. In this endurance, we choose camaraderie with God over the selfishness of gratification. But getting there is no easy task.

In order to have Faith, we have some work to do. By delving deeply into the forces that drive us we can move from merely knowing the right thing to do, to having the ability to actually carry it out with God's help. If Faith is clinging to God in the midst of desire, in the face of disappointment, without trying to control the outcome, then we must examine if we are ready for every part of it:

What do I most deeply desire?

What is and is not in my control?

How am I managing waiting and disappointment?

Am I able to receive the very thing I am asking for?

Power

I had a psychology class called "Motivation" at Purdue University. I imagined the class was going to be about what makes people tick, how they are either encouraged or discouraged, or perhaps how to inspire people. Instead, the class consisted largely of research about Pavlov's dogs and videos of caged pigeons from the 1960's. It felt disappointing - more like how to train a dog to sit and less about how to move people to tears. And yet, as I came to contemplate the fundamental lessons I was learning, the more I saw some deep truths of human nature being revealed.

At the time I took the class, the basic gist that I took away was that motivating a certain behavior (such as a mouse running through a maze) generally required some kind of favorable outcome or object (cheese at the end of the maze) related to an unmet need (hunger) that the scientists had induced (restricting the mouse's food). I didn't know it then, but I was beginning to learn how desire and suffering were related. In time, it became apparent that you cannot have one without the other. If the mouse isn't hungry, the cheese won't motivate it to run.

Our discomforts stir up our desires, and moves us to action. We can look at our discomfort through two lenses. The survival perspective only sees the agony of discomfort, and is solely interested in reducing and avoiding any pain or suffering. The thriving perspective sees goodness, and is motivated to increase delight. It's easy to have it hardwired into your mind that pain is bad and pleasure is good. Wisdom teaches us that sometimes being uncomfortable can be good, and that too much pleasure can be bad. We need more than instincts. We need the ability to perceive the goal and meaning of the forces that motivate us, and assess how they are shaping the people we are becoming as a result.

The awareness of our suffering motivates us to take care of ourselves: body, mind, and soul. Thinking that pain and suffering are only cruel is too black and white. Living in this fallen world, we use pain to help motivate us towards health, and ultimately towards God himself. That being said, pain alone is insufficient to motivate action. Hunger by itself won't drive the mouse to run through the maze. There must also be the cheese at the end of the maze. There must be hope. Without hope, discomfort becomes torturous and cruel, driving us to give up rather than to pursue health.

There is a dark side to motivation called "learned helplessness[3]." This unfortunate phenomena occurs whenever we are taught over and over that our behavior won't result in any kind of change; that no matter how hard you try, you cannot achieve your goals. Our repeated attempts teach us that we are powerless to change our circumstances, and therefore we resign ourselves completely to discomfort. Essentially, these kinds of experiences cause us to lose hope. Learned helplessness has a devastating impact on goal-seeking behavior.

In 1967, Martin Seligman conducted a rather poignant experiment about learned helplessness at the University of Pennsylvania. In his experiment, dogs were placed into two groups, both of which received electric shocks. The dogs in the first group were able to press a lever to stop the shocks, whereas the dogs in the second group could do nothing to stop them. They could only wait until the shocks randomly stopped. This part of the experiment was repeated several times, inducing a state of learned helplessness into the second group of dogs. Both groups of dogs were then taken to the same area where they were again given shocks, but could stop them by jumping over a low partition. Although the dogs from the second group could easily escape these shocks (as their circumstances had changed), they had become so conditioned to believe that nothing they could do would stop the shocks that they only laid down and whimpered when the shocks came. They had lost hope in goodness.

Humans are no different from those poor dogs. The loss of hope will keep us from doing things to help ourselves even when the answer is staring us in the face. If life has beaten us down, and we become convinced that we are powerless to change our circumstances, we give up. In fact, we are hardwired to conserve energy as a last-ditch survival strategy if we truly believe we cannot do anything else. Learned helplessness reveals a powerful truth: suffering alone does not motivate us to take action, we must also have hope.

Let's say the mouse from our earlier example is now starving. It faces a choice: to run the maze, or not. If it runs, it will use up energy faster and hasten its demise if there isn't any cheese. On the other hand, it could choose to not run and to conserve its energy, but this will guarantee its demise if the situation doesn't change. Life and death hinges upon whichever hope the mouse clings to. If the mouse believes that the cheese is gone, it will lie down and wait. We are no different when we lose hope. In other words, when we have learned that nothing we do can alleviate our suffering, we stop putting in the effort to change. When we lose hope, we give in to resignation and work to kill our own desires because they have seemingly become a waste of energy. Hopelessness considers desire as unrealistic and torturous. A chasing after the wind.

Most of us are not as far gone as complete and total learned helplessness. If anything, we more often find ourselves hovering somewhere around desperation - frantically running our mazes looking for even the tiniest morsel of cheese.

Desperation causes us to run faster and faster, terrified that if we stop, we will lose hope and crash. This is where we place our hope solely on *one* thing, such as a cup of coffee. We might think that we can function just fine... *only so long as we get that one thing.* The object of our desperation, whatever it is (money, alcohol, popularity, winning, sex, etc.), becomes our lifeline. Then, when it seems like something stands in the way of what we've come to depend on, we feel powerless and out of control. Ironically, from the outside you'll see just the opposite. We scream and demand, stomp our feet, and cause a scene to *make* life and others do exactly as we want. We look like we're on a power-trip, but internally we feel powerless, desperate, and terrified. Such behavior is ineffective. It's more likely to get you kicked out than it is to get your problems solved.

So, in sum, for us to begin seeking fulfillment we must first have an awareness of our longings, coupled with the hope that we can find resolution if we put in the effort. Ideally, that hope is placed in God, who promises us that none of our pain goes to waste. The only hope that can see us through a life of difficulty is a hope that goes beyond earthly life. On the other hand, the most miserable thing a person can experience is not having any purpose for their misery. Paul illustrates this concept in Romans 8:23-25 (NLT) when he writes about the hope of restoration:

And we believers also groan, even though we have the Holy Spirit within us as a foretaste of future glory, for we long for our bodies to be released from sin and suffering. We, too, wait with eager hope for the day when God will give us our full rights as his adopted children, including the new bodies he has promised us. We were given this hope when we were saved. (If we already have something, we don't need to hope for it. But if we look forward to something we don't yet have, we must wait patiently and confidently.)

Our groaning informs us that we are missing something. We do not suffer for things we already have. If our fulfillment were entirely within our control, we would never ache, nor have need for hope. To have hope, then, is to recognize that not only do we not have what we want, but also that we are not in complete control of getting it. Our effort is important, but doesn't guarantee a favorable outcome in this temporary, earthly life. We do know, however, that God sees the motivation of our hearts, and rewards us accordingly. No effort, whether for good or ill, will go unseen in eternity.

If our hopes are disappointed, and we decide that our efforts are pointless, and hope is only a prelude to pain, we will give in to resignation. Desperately attempting to take control over your life or abandoning any attempt to change it, is ultimately an attempt to avoid having hope and Faith. Without Faith, we come to scorn vulnerability and try to live without having to trust God or anyone else. As we defined earlier, Faith is the ability to trust God in the midst of desire, in the face of disappointment, without trying to control the outcome. However, there is one additional component. Faith chooses to focus not on the positive outcome we hope to happen, nor the negative outcome we fear will happen, but instead on having the courage to act upon the choices that are within our control. Then, we can trust God with the rest:

Shadrach, Meshach and Abednego replied to him, "King Nebuchadnezzar, we do not need to defend ourselves before you in this matter. If we are thrown into the blazing furnace, the God we serve is able to deliver us from it, and he will deliver us from Your Majesty's hand. But even if he does not, we want you to know, Your Majesty, that we will not serve your gods or worship the image of gold you have set up."

- Daniel 3:16-18 NIV

These three face their imminent deaths with straight-faced Faith. They recognize that God has free will. Although they are confident that God will rescue them, they understand that he also may not. Even still, they are motivated by their conviction to serve and worship God alone, even when it costs them their lives. They demonstrate the antithesis of learned helplessness. The choice between life and death is right before them: serve Nebuchadnezzar's gods and worship the image of gold, and they will live; refuse and they will die. They *know* they have the power to "save" themselves, and choose death rather than to betray God. They choose the flames because of what it would mean if they bowed to Nebuchadnezzar. Their conviction is that betraying God is a fate worse than death - that it is not Nebuchadnezzar who has the power of life and death, but God.

There's something else interesting about this verse. Imagine if you substituted in your idea of the modern Christian in place of Shadrach and company. I can imagine three different outcomes. First, we have the Christian who believes that everything is completely up to God, and not at all in our control or influence. This Christian has absolute assurance that God will save them, and boasts as such to the king. They have a sense of pride in their "faith," meaning that, because God is good, he will surely save them from the fire. In their mind, there's no possibility that he won't. Now, while we know that God does indeed "works for the good of those who love him" (Romans 8:28), such "faith" actually puts God to the test. *If* God is good, *then* he'll save them from the fire. And if he doesn't? Well, that's not an option. The Christian who has such a view on life only focuses on the hopeful, optimistic outcome that *they* have in mind. As a result, they set themselves up for a rude awakening along a road littered with unhelpful assumptions and judgments. For instance, they might believe that those who have bad things happen to them must have deserved it and are being punished by God.

Next is the Christian who lives in fear. They "hope" that God will save them, but, like Peter walking on the waves, their focus is really on fire. When people live in this mindset, their decisions and behavior become reactive rather than intentional and deliberate. They fixate, terrified, on the power that others have to do them harm. They desperately try to do whatever they can to avoid others' wrath. This Christian fails to focus on what is actually in their control, and only perseverates on the forces beyond their control. As such, they might come to believe that God is testing or punishing them, and that if they are good enough or beg enough, God will take the fire away. Or, they simply denounce their faith and walk away from God.

The last Christian has a similar perspective as Shadrach, Meschach, and Abednego. Their belief in God's rescue is firm, they acknowledge that God can do as he wills, and (most importantly) their focus is on the decision that is in their power: "even if he does not, we want you to know, Your Majesty, that we will *not* serve your gods or worship the image of gold..." (emphasis added). Their focus is not dead set on solely their hopeful belief, nor do they stew on the impending danger. Their emphasis is on what they will and will not do. They cannot control what the king does. They cannot completely predict what God will do. But they can decide what they will do. Now, that is not to say only "real" Christians would choose to refuse to kneel. Only that we examine what drives our decision-making. After all, perhaps God would have forgiven them for doing what it took to survive. Who is to say?

Life will bring us difficult, sometimes impossible, choices. Will we spend our lives feigning that everything will work out as we expect because we serve a God who is good? Are we in turmoil because life is full of danger? Or do we find encouragement by focusing on what we can do, limited as it may be? Such focus requires that we have an understanding of our own vulnerability, which means that we acknowledge that we are neither invulnerable, nor completely helpless. We have power, but we can also be wounded.

Living in reality is difficult. It is easier to pretend that nothing can ever hurt us, that nothing bad can possibly happen. Or, we might live thinking that life is hopelessly bad and painful, and that we are powerless to do anything about it. These pretenses are based on one common factor: that life is beyond our control and, therefore, nothing we do matters. When we imagine that we won't have to make hard decisions (or that we cannot do so), it protects us from the pain and responsibility when things don't go our way. Life is neither entirely in our control (we cannot make life wholly safe), and neither is it completely outside of our control. Thus, in order to have genuine Faith we must be ready to deal with the consequences and responsibilities of our own decision making.

We think we want power in life, but at almost every opportunity we try to surrender that which gives us the most power - the power of choice.

We want our decisions to be obvious, or for someone else to make decisions for us. We plead that we don't know what to do if the decisions we're faced with are ambiguous, difficult, or carry significant consequences. Having to make decisions, and bear the consequences of those choices, terrifies us. It seems easier, by far, if we deceive ourselves into thinking we can blame others or claim innocence for negative outcomes. Choices expose us. Our character is revealed in our decision making process: what we want, why we want it, and (most importantly) how we try to obtain what we want.

We need to examine how we make decisions: what thought processes, motivations, fears, and desires guide us when we're faced with choices. Life will inherently force us into positions where we must make decisions. It can be scary making decisions, especially when the pressure's on. We worry about making the wrong choice and hurting ourselves or those around us. But, as we've covered, pain in life is inevitable. It is better to decide what is worth a little pain in our lives than it is to try to avoid any pain at all.

Living with Faith and vulnerability doesn't guarantee us that we won't be hurt. If anything, Faith recognizes the possibility that we might be hurt, and has come to accept that reality. Faith doesn't concern itself with avoiding hurt, but focuses instead on what we do with that hurt. Our confidence does not come from imagining that we will never be hurt, but that we are capable of being healed from every wound. Choosing to take heart in that truth is what's left to us.

Disappointment

I submit to your consideration that the single greatest mark of maturity is the ability to manage disappointment well. When we are young, we are hardwired to expect the world to conform to our whims. When things go awry, children the world around will fuss and throw fits because they have yet to master the ability to soothe themselves. Sadly, some never gain mastery over their disappointment. Instead, they hide their inability to cope with their vulnerability behind a wall of denial or justification - that if others were more competent or if the world were more fair, then they wouldn't feel so miserable.

How do you respond when you cannot have what you want? Will

you attempt to take what you want by force? Perhaps in the pain of your disappointment you'll attempt to convince yourself and others that you never cared about it in the first place. Consider for a moment how the people you know respond when things don't pan out as they had hoped. How do your friends and family react when they don't get their way?

Ideally, as we develop we are taught how to endure disappointment. All too often, however, we are taught the exact opposite. Some of us never taste disappointment because our families spoil and enable us - doing whatever it takes to quell our tantrums. Obviously, this breeds entitlement within us, causing us to explode when things don't go as we anticipated because we've never had to deal with disappointment. On the other hand, we might be punished for voicing our disappointment and frustration. This kind of influence replaces the honest struggle with disappointment for silence bred from fear. When we are raised this way, we don't learn how to deal with disappointment; we learn how to hide it. Our parental figures may have been good examples and teachers, or they may have made it more difficult for us to cope with not having control. In either case, as we grow up we each become responsible for learning how to endure setbacks.

We perseverate in our anger and disappointments not because life is out of our control, but because our internal life is out of our control. We don't know how to manage our disappointments well, and instead project our need for control on the world around us. When we are aggravated or grieved by the way events unfold, we must set aside the external factors and take the introspective journey to distill the true nature of what is bothering us. It is in these deep, innermost places where our hurts can be healed. Or, they can be left to fester, which drives us to self-protect rather than self-understand. We must venture into the difficulty if we are to grow beyond it.

Few things in life are as difficult as the feelings that stem from rejection, especially when we're beginning to take risks by being vulnerable. When our hopes don't become our reality, we may come to be angry with God, believing that he has betrayed us. We may think that we know what we need more than God does. Because we believe that God is all powerful, it is easy to see disappointment as betrayal or rejection from God. Betrayal holds anger against God, but rejection holds anger towards ourselves. It is easy for the feeling of rejection to turn into the feeling of shame. Our shame causes us to fixate on ourselves: what we are doing wrong, or the notion that we somehow *are* wrong. Rejection, and the shame it so often creates, can make us believe that we are better off hiding from others and our hurts. We come to believe that it is better to not be open than it is to be rejected again.

But closing ourselves off only guarantees perpetual disappointment. Because of repeated disappointments, we come to believe that our desires and relationships are dangerous and that fulfillment is unattainable. We turn to Apathy and hopelessness to make sense of our despondency. Therefore, we avoid honest dialogue about our feelings, no matter whether our feelings are positive or negative. We treat our own desires as a setup for disappointment. Apathy is the ultimate learned helplessness and results in massive amputations to the heart - we kill off the part of ourselves that wants things to be better, so as to avoid being hurt further.

If hope were indeed futile, Apathy wouldn't be a bad coping mechanism. However, the truth of it is that God wants to be our unshakeable hope, that we might turn to him even when it feels pointless to try. Because, eventually, God *will* come through. Imagine if, before the creation of Eve, Adam had turned to Apathy to cope with his loneliness. Upon seeing Eve for the first time, rather than exclaiming, "Bone of my bones and flesh of my flesh!" he might have simply told God, "Thanks, but I don't care anymore." Once we have eliminated our desire and hope, fulfillment becomes irrelevant. We guarantee our own disappointment. When we become Apathetic, God may bless us but we are not led to gratitude because we've simply stopped caring. All because of a misplaced attempt to stop hurting. When we deny our pains, we also surrender the fulfillment that follows.

Such Apathy is merely one way of hiding our disappointment. Unfortunately, there are far more ways that we come to believe we must hide our feelings than there are invitations to vulnerable honesty. We cannot wait for life to roll out the red carpet for our hope. No, we have to blaze new trails through the wilderness and wreckage in our hearts. We accept the difficulty that we'd rather not have to deal with. If we cannot accept the possibility of disappointment, then we will eventually kill off our hope in order to compensate.

If you tell a child that they cannot have some toy they found while you are shopping together, you're likely to encounter a tantrum. The child lacks the ability to cope with disappointment. The child might beg, cry, and shout. They might even ask unhelpful questions, like, "But *why* can't I have it?!" Answering that question won't help them. What will help them is learning how to trust and consider what power they have to work towards the things they want. A helpful adult might come alongside the child, help them to recognize their feelings and where they're coming from, then work with them to accept and manage that disappointment. Perhaps they'll make a plan for how the child can get the toy in the future if they save up money or help with chores.

If only we all had people in our lives that taught us to manage our internal worlds instead of making demands of the external world. Perhaps we would all be better able to live and risk boldly, rather than spending our time and energy trying to avoid disappointment. It seems more common that, when we are children, the people in our lives punish us for our inability to cope with disappointment rather than help us to learn how to deal with it. All too often we are influenced to hide and avoid disappointment; not because of the disappointment itself, but because when we are disappointed we don't know how to move beyond it.

We do so because we believe that our disappointment is pointless and unmanageable, or that we will be punished for showing it. We need to rewire our notions of disappointment, and the difficult emotions that it can create. We need to hear: "It's okay to be disappointed. It's okay to feel it and I want you to tell me about it. I know it hurts right now, you don't need to hide it. I'm here. Let's get through this together. Will you trust me?"

Disappointments are not a sign that you are bad or immature. It's okay to feel disappointment and all that comes with it. Never feeling disappointed, hurt, angry, or let down isn't a sign of maturity, but of a heart that's given up. Neither is it mature to cause a scene when we're upset. Maturity comes as we develop relational trust in God that allows us to make courageous decisions to be vulnerable about our feelings, desires, and disappointments. In fact, disappointment (in moderation), is actually a sign of a healthy relationship.

You cannot have an authentic relationship with someone who always says "yes" to you. On the other hand, constant rejection is also a problem. God neither constantly rejects us, nor always heeds us. And this is good for us. A complex, real relationship is fulfilling, but it's also risky. To be yourself in an authentic relationship means that the other person also has the freedom to be true to themselves. There's bound to be some disagreements when two people are free to be honest with one another.

We find fulfillment by living in an intimate, authentic relationship with God in all his wildness. In this relationship, when we are disappointed, our frustrated longings remind us that we are living with God authentically. Fulfillment in God is worth the risk of disappointment. And when we do happen to find momentary fulfillment, we know that it is a gift from God. Moreover, whether we find or not, we come to know that God is always available to us. It is not the momentary pleasures of life that satisfy us, but knowledge of God's constant care for us. In God's constant availability we find the lasting fulfillment we most deeply long for. Paul learned something similar to this, and remarked of the difference it made in his life in Philippians 4:11-13 NIV:

> *I have learned to be content whatever the circumstances. I know what it is to be in need, and I know what it is to have plenty. I have learned the secret of being content in any and every situation, whether well fed or hungry, whether living in plenty or in want. I can do all this through him who gives me strength.*

Few of us struggle to be content when our circumstances are favorable. It's in the moments of unmet desire where our perception of God's goodness becomes challenged, which really is only an outcome of how well we are able to manage our disappointment. If you need any further examination of this dilemma, just flip to the book of Job. It is difficult to maintain the notion of God's goodness when we are suffering. On the other hand, gratified desire doesn't guarantee that we will easily trust God either. Even when our desires are fulfilled through Faith, in this life there will be some sense of sadness and loss. Even the birth of a child brings about the loss of something of the former life up till then. The human heart doesn't come equipped to handle the constantly changing world. When we look for comfort in the world, it will elude us, and only frustrate us further. Rather, to manage disappointment, we must look to master that which is in our control: ourselves.

Control

The problem isn't if you'll experience disappointment, but what you'll do when it inevitably happens. Our culture doesn't do well with not getting what we want. Society has become more and more oriented around instant gratification; desiring life to go exactly as we expect without having to exert much effort at all. We want to feel like we are the ones in control, and capable of managing the world around us. However, human beings are fundamentally vulnerable, and therefore, we lack the control we like to imagine we have. We expend energy trying to change the world, and not enough energy trying to change ourselves.

It's easy to be tricked into thinking that we have control when we are able to take what we want. If I throw a bag of popcorn in the microwave and come back a minute or two later to find it cooked to perfection, I might think that *I* am the one in control. "Look at what I can do with the simple push of a button!" Over time, we become deceived into believing that we have total control and become woefully unprepared when reality sets in. Maybe the grocery store runs out of popcorn, it goes stale, the bag rips open, the power goes out, or the popcorn gets overcooked. Likely, you did not sow the corn, water it, harvest it, package it, set up the electricity grid, make a microwave oven, and program its timer. You pressed a button or two. I hope you see the point. The popcorn is *least of all* in our control, and more in the control of a thousand other factors beyond our control. But it's easier to huff and puff when it goes wrong than it is to acknowledge how little control we really have. Anger gives us the illusion of power when we are dwarfed by life's chaos.

When we pursue the fulfillment of some desire, it is the combination of a few limited factors within our control and countless factors beyond our control coming together. What we do control is quite small, but still significant: Will we *try* to find fulfillment? Are we willing to do our part, however small or large it might be? Even if you're locked in a padded cell in a straight jacket, the choice of whether or not you will try to break out remains up to you. No one can make you not try except yourself. However, whether you actually break out or not is *not* within your complete control.

To some extent or another, we are dependent on factors beyond our influence working out favorably. Understandably then, it's easy to fall into the trap of trying to control those external factors as much as possible. In this way, relationship with God becomes more about appeasing him than it does offering him your heart. But this is really only an attempt to control God, and everyone else. This effort proves disastrous.

Consider how you respond when others try to control you, manipulate you, threaten you, or tell you what to do. You resist it. You fight back. Everyone does; at least at first. Trying to force our way through life, we only make it harder on ourselves and everyone around us. Truthfully, the more desperately we try to control things beyond ourselves, the more out of control we really become. And therefore, more desperate, more toxic.

As soon as we give into the alternatives of trusting God, we lose our control. We will either be ruled by God and self-control, or sin and the enemy.

Jesus replied, "Very truly I tell you, everyone who sins is a slave to sin.
- John 8:34 NIV

When we believe that it is better to sin than to risk disappointment, it is like the enemy has a signed contract that our longings are his to do with as he pleases. We are slaves not to our desires themselves, but to whom we have given over control of those desires. The same longing may draw one person to love their spouse selflessly, and another to an affair. It is what we *do* with our desires that makes the difference. What we choose to do with our desires is always our choice alone. It is where we have control. Your temptations don't define you. What you choose to do with those temptations, however, does.

And so that's exactly where the enemy will attack - your identity and your sense of control. When we believe our desires and temptations define us, that we are powerless over them, we forfeit the one place where we have control. We begin to give in, and the feeling of powerlessness grows. As the tendency to indulge in sin deepens, its influence leads us to conclude that it would be an unbearable torment were we to resist. We come to believe that it is better to sin with the devil than to ache with God. We are convinced that we are incapable of resisting sin and temptation. We learn to be helpless.

It is a lie.

However feeble it might seem, we can always resist. In fact, scripture promises:

Submit yourselves, then, to God. Resist the devil, and he will flee from you. Come near to God and he will come near to you.
- *James 4:7-8a NIV*

It is easier to feign that we don't have any control over our lives, or desperately try to scoop up all control, than it is to acknowledge what is actually in our control. Vulnerability is hard. It's tempting to think that we cannot be blamed, or conclude that it's somehow all our fault. We like to think we live in a predictable world, or we else abdicate any responsibility at all. When our expectations and our reality are different, we are quick to either look for something or someone to blame, or take all of the blame ourselves. In fact, I believe that we all start with blame when we are disappointed. We try to figure out who has control, but we typically come to unhelpful answers. After all, what is denial, anger, and bargaining if not an attempt to pin blame on someone? The progression of our inner dialogue when we're disappointed is almost predictable.

"I'm sure everything's fine."

"What do you mean it's not fine?!"

"If I (or "you") hadn't been such an idiot, everything would have been fine."

"You (or "I") can't do *anything* right."

Notice the extremes. It's all either okay, or entirely not okay. It's all our fault, or not our fault at all. The difficulty is determining the nuanced responsibility we actually bear when we are disappointed. The truth is that we are partly in control. But we get stuck trying to assign blame and miss working through the actual problem - our disappointment. We will heal more when we concern ourselves less with uncovering why things happened, and more concerned about what we will do with what has already happened. We have control over the decision of what we will do with our disappointment. Assigning blame is only an attempt to deny our disappointment, and only perpetuates feeling out of control.

Let's say that life's disappointments and wounds are like getting hit by an arrow. The pain of this experience might drive us to begin firing back our own arrows in an effort to protect ourselves from further harm. Or perhaps we take another route, running away and cowering for fear of getting struck again. Either way, life quickly becomes defined by fear, manifesting in either hostility or avoidance. All the while, the arrow is still digging in, causing you pain.

These strategies only manage the external realities of life. It projects the internal wound onto the external world, and thus tries to make the world more tame or distant so as to not reawaken the unaddressed wound. But these strategies fail. We cannot make our pain less by denying it or inflicting pain onto others. Even finding a place to hide won't mitigate the dangers of life. Hiding and fighting only make the suffering worse. We cannot control whether or not we get struck by arrows. We only control how we'll respond and what we'll do with the arrows already stuck in us. If we fail to address the arrows already lodged in us, the inevitable arrows that follow become more severe in our minds as a result of our insistence to never be hurt again.

Learning to appropriately address our arrows doesn't come easily. In fact, if we're not careful, we might inflict further harm on ourselves as we try to dig the arrows out. But what matters is that we're trying to deal with what's in our control. And, eventually, with the right knowledge, skills, and help, we can find healing for arrows both old and new. The journey to find healing, and the freedom that follows, grants us confidence to face life in all its beauty and danger. That confidence doesn't come from an inflated sense of control, nor by avoidance, but by the quiet fortitude earned through healing. Hope, peace, and confidence aren't gained through invulnerability, but by the conviction that all wounds can be healed. Only then can we continue in courageous vulnerability.

Be like a rocky promontory against which the restless surf continually pounds; it stands fast while the churning sea is lulled to sleep at its feet. I hear you say, "How unlucky that this should happen to me!" Not at all! Say instead, "How lucky that I am not broken by what has happened and am not afraid of what is about to happen. The same blow might have struck anyone, but not many would have absorbed it without capitulation or complaint."

-Marcus Aurelius[4]

When disappointment exposes our lack of control, we can plead that life is unfair and cruel. We might continue trying to assert control over the "restless surf" that torments us, or give up any hope of relief. Or, we can take the courageous, difficult path towards Faith; where we must come to acknowledge that we have control, however limited it may be. Our control isn't primarily concerned with what happens to us, but what we do with what has happened - how we manage our waiting, disappointment, and fulfillment.

God desires to be a part of those processes. We are given every assurance that we not only *can* come to God in the midst of our waiting, disappointment, and fulfillment, but that we are also *encouraged* to do so.

Be anxious for nothing, but in everything, by prayer and petition, with thanksgiving, present your requests to God. And the peace of God, which surpasses all understanding, will guard your hearts and your minds in Christ Jesus.

- Philippians 4:6-7 NIV

Do we, "in everything," bring our requests before God?

I contend that the point of coming to God with prayer, petition, thanksgiving, and requests is not about a duty to inform God of *everything*, but instead about intimacy: coming before God with the burdens and cares of your heart. God wants to be part of our lives. No desire or request is too much for God to handle, but we must also recognize God's power by submitting to his will. Even Jesus, when he was praying about his coming death, had the audacity to go before God with his desires that he knew may have been out of bounds with God's ultimate will.

The situation can seem stacked against us when we try to remain patient as we wait upon God in Faith. We can remain faithful, patient, and hopeful, but that means we may suffer agony while we wait. Or, our own insistence in getting our way can tempt us into finding the shortcuts to "relief." This internal tug-of-war divides us: a part of us longs to do the right thing and another longs only for gratification. Faith requires the commitment to remain obedient to God, whereas in indulgence we acquiesce to the illusion of relief. We all struggle with the tension between waiting in Faith and the temptation to take "control." Thank goodness, then, that life presents us with situations that are beyond our control, where we don't even have to face this problem.

For instance, we can do nothing about whether or not there is an afterlife. We can only take it in faith because it is completely outside of our control. We have no say in the matter, and only have the option of whether or not to have faith. We cannot construct our own afterlife. The alternative is grueling. There are situations where, rather than being completely out of our control and having to rely on faith, we recognize we have the choice to take control. The forbidden fruit lies within our grasp, and we have the choice whether or not we will take it.

Most people think that they want power and control, but few things are more terrifying. God gives us a massive responsibility: the power to choose. How often do we say, "I'd do anything for you," without considering the weight of those words. Would you really? On the surface, it might sound nice, but doing anything for someone makes them your god. We must learn to appropriately wield our power of choice. When wielded appropriately, the power of choice gives us a sense of self-control and peace. Learning to live in that power, and surrender it to God when necessary, is the hard part.

If we refuse to neither control ourselves nor have Faith in God, we will become ruled by discomfort. Life will be reduced to only being concerned about how we can escape pain. We lose control of ourselves and lose touch with God. Instead of having self-control and vulnerability with God, we demand that we should not have to ache, especially when we want something. Opposed to our longings taking us closer to God as they ought, Greed and Manipulation demand that we never risk the vulnerability inherent in entrusting others. These alternatives entangle us in a dangerous web. If we're left to Manipulation and Greed for too long, we'll eventually succumb to a sense of insecurity and futility (respectively), which drive us to Apathy. In Apathy, we encounter the complete loss of Faith and of the last vestiges of self-control.

We must combat insecurity with vulnerability, and futility with self-control. By boldly entrusting God with our hopes and doing our part in managing ourselves and our choices, we choose Faith. The path to finding fulfillment in and with God is a hard road, especially when we are accustomed to either vain attempts of control, or capitulation to hopelessness. We know there will be pain and discomfort along the way. Waiting and trusting is work. Luckily, we do not walk the road alone. Jesus is intimately aware of our pain, and if we turn to him he *will* heal us in his time and in his way. He will remove and heal the arrows we don't know what to do with. His healing gives us the confidence we need to live in this dangerous world with vulnerability and Faith.

The Christian life is meant to be lived in an authentic relationship with God. It is vulnerable and trusting, and therefore open to the possibility that God might not answer us in the ways we want. Asking and submitting our requests to God means that we recognize who has control over what. We have control over where we take our search for fulfillment and how we respond to its conclusion, and God controls the rest. Understanding that doesn't mean dealing with adversity will be any easier, but it does change the meaning of adversity. Rather than only seeing difficulty as problematic and uncomfortable, we begin to see it as the crucible that fortifies our Faith, intimacy, and vulnerability. It grows us, and our relationship and security with God deeps as a result.

Suffering Reinterpreted

A young woman I worked with once told me a curious story. She explained that she went on a date with a new guy, and that it went alright. But it was just alright. Her date was polite, but too deferential. After the date, she thanked him, but told him with courage and kindness that she was not interested in a second date. Why? Because he was being too nice. In our conversation, she observed that her date seemed to be avoiding any kind of disagreement, veiled as being "nice," rather than just being himself.

When two people are both free to be true to their unique selves they will have conflict. But the kind of conflict that arises from people being authentic is worth it, especially if we know how to manage and resolve conflict well. In the same way, we will have conflicts with God because God wants a real relationship with us. He is uninterested in lip service that conceals a broken heart. Rather, he looks for men and women who can be honest; who bring their heart before God. There's nothing noble about acting like you're not suffering or disappointed when in fact you are.

We mistakenly believe that relationships are healthy when there isn't conflict or difficulty. Relationships, even our relationship with God, become strengthened when we work through difficulty together with courage and mutual respect. There cannot be any growth if we're surrounded by sycophants. We need the crucible of differing agendas, opinions, and viewpoints, lest we become dogmatic in all our beliefs. Conflict between two people can help them come to a better understanding of one another. Similarly, when we are disappointed, it can foster a deeper awareness of ourselves and intimacy with God. Seen this way, suffering becomes something that is neither avoided nor exacerbated. Instead, our suffering is held lightly while it is present, and appreciated as a catalyst for our growth.

In the midst of enduring suffering, if we search our hearts we will find that what we truly hope for is God and his love. This awareness shifts our desire from the object of our desires to the one who gives it. We have hobbies because they help us to connect to others who share our same interests, not merely because we enjoy the hobby itself. In fact, when "enjoyed" alone, most everything loses its shine.

In this season of life, I enjoy sneaking down to the local creek and going fly fishing. Taking friends and family with me is a lot of fun - I enjoy sharing the experience and seeing their delight when they make a catch. But there are also times when I want to be by myself on the water. If I'm being honest, going fishing by myself isn't really about seeking isolation, as if such a thing were even possible. There's a common saying that goes, "Fishing isn't about catching." There's a lot of truth in that statement, and it goes further. Fishing (or anything we do for that matter) is not about what you see on the surface.

I think most people, Christian or not, pursue God without knowing it. We go fishing "by ourselves" thinking that we are getting "alone time." It's nonsense. We aren't really seeking after fish, or trees, or vacation, or mountains, or beaches, or any other earthly thing. Our core desire is to encounter God and his love. And when we consciously realize that, things begin to make a lot more sense.

Our desires are meant to bring us closer to others, and especially to God. (Addiction and manipulation believe the opposite, hence why they are unhealthy. They prioritize the experiential opportunity over the relational opportunity. Think someone who is more interested in a concert than in sharing the experience of the concert with the people they go with.) Even though God is not present to us in the flesh, being mindful of God and inviting him into our experiences makes what we are doing far more meaningful.

When you're walking through the woods,

Looking out over a city,

Driving through the country,

Admiring a sunset,

Or watching your favorite movie,

Remember and delight in the one who created it all.

If we only resign ourselves to a passing observation of beauty, without "stopping and smelling the roses," our participation and relationship with Jesus loses its vibrancy. Vivid spirituality becomes sterile and fails to capture our imaginations and our hearts. We begin to presume that God is insufficient to fill the hole in our hearts. Making God ordinary may make God seem easier to approach or comprehend, but we lose sight of his nature. We make God "nice," and so our hearts are not captured by him. Neither do we need to dramatize God (if such a thing is even possible). God is enough.

God is a fierce and bold lover. His affection, beauty, and glory are proclaimed in the majesty of the stars, the serenity of an ocean beach, and in the treasures of our most intimate relationships. Yet we so often relegate God's love for us to cognitive and religious terms that fail to move us. We put God in a box. Our refusal to be vulnerable with God, to open up about what we most deeply long for, sabotages everything we profess to hold dear.

The reality of it is that these moments of beauty, however good and lovely, are inconsistent. Sometimes the fish don't bite. When I summited my first mountain, a cold front moved through and covered the mountaintop in fog, obscuring the view. If we only look for goodness from the experience itself, we'll wind up frustrated. But when the *shared* experience is the source of our fulfillment, then no matter what happens we'll have a story to tell. After all, which is more interesting? The story where everything goes according to plan, or the one where there are unexpected twists and challenges? We prefer the latter, so long as it's someone else's story. Why? I think it's because when we face adversity, we don't look at it as ourselves and God off on an adventure. Instead, we see problems as only miserable and as a sign of someone's failure. Problems make us feel alone and exposed. When we live in the awareness of God's company, however, things begin to change.

If inviting God into our moments of delight makes the experience richer and more meaningful, then the same can be true of our moments of pain. When we invite God into the midst of our suffering and disappointment, it changes our beliefs about adversity. Whenever we suffer and search for God despite our pain, we get a taste of God's heart for us - his love and care for humanity. In the midst of our longings, we preview how much more God longs for us. When we understand the lengths that God went to for us, we come to appreciate our longings as echoes of his longing and pursuit of us.

Let me say, however, that this thought is not meant to permit you to stir up idolatrous desire and excuse it as some act of holiness by equating it with experiencing God's love or desire. This is by no means a call to indulge in revelry and excuse indulgence as "experiencing God." The purpose here is to understand, to some degree, God's heart towards us as we suffer in and for goodness. Impure desire cannot possibly lead us to Christ. We must examine our motives. Are we entertaining greedy desires and justifying it with "righteous" excuses, or living by our convictions and drawing closer to God when it becomes difficult?

When used appropriately, learning to appreciate our desires and disappointments as shared experiences with God makes us more resilient in our Faith. For instance, when we feel rejected, the sting can become to us a reminder of how often people have rejected God as he longs for us. So, although we hurt because of the rejection, we still cling to God. Our Faith deepens. The longings we feel, which we believe are *unbearable,* are only a pinprick compared to God's desire for us. The longings we feel can become a reminder that brings us closer to God's heart: God longs for you more than you long for anything else in this world.

Our desires and disappointments are the catalysts that either draw us closer to God, or drive us further apart. In disappointment, just as in desire, we can choose to draw closer to others or to withdraw away from them. Disappointment may cause us to come to doubt that God *really* means to do us good, and so we give in to Manipulation, Greed, or Apathy to protect ourselves from further pain and disappointment.

Suffering must be carefully interpreted if we are to manage it properly in order to maintain Faith. This means that we have to slow down when we're upset - which is the very opposite of what we feel like doing when we're anything other than happy. We try to skip to the end step of processing, where we can find some reasonable conclusion to make sense of our discontent. We cannot afford to minimize our hurts and hope they'll magically go away. Our wounds require careful consideration and recourse. It's easier to blame ourselves for not doing or knowing enough, or others for being incompetant or cruel, than it is to get to the real source of our pain. But life is too nuanced to be solved by blame alone. The issues that drive our angst are never the topical sources we generally credit, but rather the core cares and concerns buried deep within us. Getting down to those depths takes some work, but need not intimidate us.

There are many pathways to healing. As a counselor, I'm constantly kept on my toes by the complexity of the human heart. There is no "one size fits all" approach to dealing with our wounds and scars. Even if you find something that works for you personally, it might be effective in one instance, but not in another. I believe that this is in large part due to God wanting to be our Healer. He wants us to come to him with our hurts, not follow a step-by-step guide.

Like falling in love, there aren't instructions to follow for finding healing. That being said, there are certain themes and patterns that can either help or hinder. Dealing with our suffering and getting to the core of it requires patience, honesty, curiosity, courage, hope, and love. If we insist on relief, try to rush through the process, harbor self-loathing, deny our problems, blame our circumstances, or seek vengeance, we will stand in our own way. We must take our story, our pain, and our hearts seriously.

Let's consider the disciple Peter as a case study for how to work through suffering in a way that deepens Faith. Check out his take on suffering after spending his life with Christ and witnessing his crucifixion and resurrection:

"Dear friends, do not be surprised at the painful trial you are suffering, as though something strange were happening to you. But rejoice that you participate in the sufferings of Christ, so that you may be overjoyed when his glory is revealed."

- 1 Peter 4:12-13 NIV

Are Peter's words disruptive to you? When I stop to think about it, the notion of rejoicing in suffering seems outlandish and perhaps even offensive. Surely if someone were to come to you in the midst of your suffering and tell you to not be surprised but to rejoice, you'd think of them as an insensitive jerk! How dare Peter to tell us to rejoice in our suffering? And he doesn't say it just once; he seems almost obsessed with the idea:

"...though now for a little while you may have had to suffer grief in all kinds of trials. These have come so that your faith - of greater worth than gold, which perishes even though refined by fire - may be proved genuine and may result in praise, glory, and honor when Jesus Christ is revealed."
- 1 Peter 1:6b-7 NIV

"For it is commendable if a man bears up under the pain of unjust suffering because he is conscious of God. But how is it to your credit if you receive a beating for doing wrong and endure it? But if you suffer for doing good and you endure it, this is commendable before God. To this you were called, because Christ suffered for you, leaving you an example, that you should follow in his steps."
- 1 Peter 1:19-21 NIV

"So then, since Christ suffered physical pain, you must arm yourselves with the same attitude he had, and be ready to suffer, too. For if you have suffered physically for Christ, you have finished with sin."
- 1 Peter 4:1 NLT

"So then, those who suffer according to God's will should commit themselves to their faithful Creator and continue to do good."
- 1 Peter 4:19 NIV

Peter is dead set on redefining the way we handle our suffering. It sounds counterintuitive... until we consider Peter's story.

Jesus first found Simon Peter early on in the gospels as a simple fisherman. Jesus was in Simon's boat, teaching to a crowd of people standing on the shore. When he was finished teaching, Jesus told Simon to let down the nets for a catch of fish and, wouldn't you know it, he hauled in the biggest catch of his life! Simon knew that he was dealing with a holy man. He fell to his knees and begged for Jesus to leave him be, because he knew that he was a sinful man. But Jesus encouraged him. Jesus called him to become a "fisher of men," and changed his name from Simon to Peter.

For the next few years, Peter and the other disciples traveled the countryside, climbed mountains, sailed seas with Jesus. They fed a throng with only a few fish and a couple loaves of bread. The disciples watched Jesus debate with the religious authorities, and heal those suffering from disabilities. Even when many of the disciples abandoned Jesus, Peter held fast:

"You do not want to leave too, do you?" Jesus asked the Twelve. Simon Peter answered him, "Lord, to whom shall we go? You have the words of eternal life. We have come to believe and to know that you are the Holy One of God."
- John 6:67-69 NIV

Peter was loyal to Jesus, and committed himself to him. Then, a fateful day came when Jesus was arrested and taken right out of their midst. Just moments before, Peter had boasted to Jesus that he would go with him to prison and even to certain death. But Jesus tells Peter that he will deny him three times. After Jesus was arrested, Peter secretly followed Jesus from a distance as a mob took Jesus to the religious and legal authorities.

Peter was recognized as he was following the crowd. But, to his shame, he gave into fear and denied association with Jesus three times. Just as Jesus told him he would. After the third time, scripture says that Peter, "went outside and wept bitterly," (Luke 22:62). Peter was nowhere to be seen when Jesus perished on the cross - scripture doesn't make it clear where he is. Perhaps he is there, watching at a distance, or maybe he was far off. After Jesus died and was entombed, Peter went into hiding with the other disciples.

I wonder what must have been going on within Peter's heart and mind during those three days after Jesus' death, before the resurrection. Perhaps he thought that it was all for nothing, that everything was over and ruined. The disciples thought that Jesus was going to restore the kingdom of Israel in dramatic fashion, but instead he was brutally executed. And it ended horribly for Peter. He blew it. He boasted that he would never abandon Jesus, and then almost immediately afterwards, he betrayed him and seemingly left him alone to die. The shame, guilt, and fear must have been overwhelming. *Everything* that he had come to know over the past few years, everything that made him "Peter," was gone. Hope was lost. The savior was dead.

Except the story wasn't over.

On the third day after Jesus' death, Peter heard a strange report from a couple of women who were attending Jesus' tomb. They told the disciples about Jesus' tomb being open, his body missing, and angels proclaiming to them that Jesus was alive. While the other disciples dismissed the women, Peter and John took off running for the tomb. They didn't find the angels or Jesus, but Peter went into the empty tomb and saw Jesus' burial linens. He went away wondering, hoping beyond hope that maybe, just maybe, Jesus was back.

Some time later, Peter and the other disciples went back to their old lives, fishing on the Sea of Galilee. It had been a long night, and they hadn't caught a thing. The following morning, a distant figure on the beach asked them if they had caught anything. "No," they replied sourly. The person on the beach told them to lower their nets for a catch on the other side of their boat. Even though they were discouraged, they decided to let down their nets one last time... and they made a catch so huge that they were unable to haul it in. They knew what this meant. It was a sign that only these fishermen, who had been with Jesus since the beginning, would understand.

John told Peter, "It is the Lord!" and Peter didn't wait for the boat to get to shore. He jumped overboard and swam headlong to where Jesus was waiting with breakfast ready to serve. They ate, then Jesus invited Peter for a walk. Peter had to have known this was coming. It was the dreaded, "we need to talk," moment. I imagine his stomach must have been in knots. Jesus walked with Peter, and reinstated him. Peter had denied Jesus three times, and now Jesus had Peter affirm three times that he loved him. (See John ch. 21)

Not only was Jesus back from the dead, but Peter himself was restored. His mistakes were not the final word. Time and time again, Peter witnessed Jesus defy the odds and come through after everyone else had given up. This is the same Peter who admonishes us to delight in our suffering, so long as our suffering is a result of doing good and in faith of God. Peter was living proof of Jesus' words in John 16:20-22 (ESV):

Truly, truly, I say to you, you will weep and lament, but the world will rejoice. You will be sorrowful, but your sorrow will turn into joy. When a woman is giving birth, she has sorrow because her hour has come, but when she has delivered the baby, she no longer remembers the anguish, for joy that a human being has been born into the world. So also you have sorrow now, but I will see you again, and your hearts will rejoice, and no one will take your joy from you.

Peter, who betrayed Jesus and was left feeling guilty and hopeless, earned the right to say that we should rejoice in our sorrow. He witnessed death and shame being defeated. He tasted first-hand the faithfulness of God even when all seemed lost. Peter understood that God comes through when everything else fails. As a result, his writing demonstrates his stubborn assurance that God will work all things out to the benefit of those who love him. He had seen that very truth play out in his own life.

Peter knew that when we are suffering, goodness is right over the horizon. If we remain faithful in God throughout the course of suffering, we *will* experience the love of God. In other words, Peter knows that all suffering really is, for the faithful, is a groaning anticipation for God to come through.

...we also glory in our sufferings, because we know that suffering produces perseverance; perseverance, character; and character, hope. And hope does not put us to shame, because God's love has been poured out into our hearts through the Holy Spirit, who has been given to us.

- Romans 5:3-4 NIV

As Christians, we have a hope that cannot be disappointed - cannot be put to shame. We have a hope that survives any disappointment. This hope is not only the promise of eternal life, but also of God's abundant love, which is always available to us. If we train ourselves to look for it, we will find that God loves us in very real, tangible, and personal ways. Like he did with Peter, Jesus finds us in ways that are unique to our relationship with him. He reminds us that we are treasured, honored, and sought after.

Rich experiences with God are not reserved for some holy sect of super-Christians. Real encounters with God, experiences that resonate with the deepest parts of ourselves, are what we pursue; not copy-cat religious practices, nor the grind of daily life. We crave real relationship with a real God. The one who knows us inside and out. The only one who can speak to our soul.

And although God will come to us in times of beauty, delight, and comfort, we know deep down that our hearts are truly won over when God comes through for us in times of darkness, suffering, and despair. Living in anticipation of God's redemption we no longer see our suffering as overwhelming and miserable, but as a herald of impending goodness. This confidence gives us the courage to endure in hope and Faith.

We are made to hope for God's power, eager to see him overcome the difficulty surrounding us. We especially desire to see him conquer the pain within us. We yearn to be overcome by his goodness. And yet, we hesitate to receive him in the midst of our pain. We want to be healed and redeemed, but come to dread the savior that hurdles the defenses we've erected to keep ourselves safe. Healing requires naming the suffering we typically prefer to deny. To invite Christ into our suffering, we must eventually enter the places in our hearts we want to close off: the dark recesses of our hearts where we hold our deepest hurt and shame.

Honor

March in Indiana is a peculiar month. The weather can shift from freezing rain to warm, sunny skies, then back again in an instant. Be that as it may, one weekend in March, my wife and I caught a rare, warm weekend. The birds were singing, there was a light breeze, and the sky was dotted with puffy white clouds. We decided to spend the morning in our backyard, laying in hammocks with a couple of good books, sometimes closing them to look up and enjoy the weather. Around lunchtime, we caught the scent of a grill drifting over from the neighbor's, and we knew we had to follow suit. We hadn't yet stocked up on our normal barbequing food, so I promptly went to the grocery store to pick up hotdogs, buns, and strawberries.

When I got back, we had a wonderful, lazy afternoon. I grilled while my wife swayed in her hammock, and once the food was cooked I went inside to prep our meal. The hotdogs were a bit charred (apparently my skill as a grillsman had waned over the winter), so I chose the two that were a bit less burnt for my wife. I was working to stuff one of them into a hotdog bun when the bun tore in two and sent the hotdog rolling across our not-entirely-clean kitchen counter. Without so much as a single thought I corralled the rogue hotdog and, as best as I could, sandwiched it back into the mangled bun.

As I was applying the condiments, I sensed God's prompting: "You could take that hotdog, and give her one of the other ones you have. " But I dismissed the thought and justified to myself that I had already defined *this* hotdog as *her* hotdog.

But then God came back with, "You didn't even wipe off the hotdog after it rolled across the counter."

I pretended like I wasn't listening. No big deal. It's only a hotdog. I'm sure she won't mind. After all, I'm the one who made the food, so it should be my decision who eats what. It's fine.

I'm ashamed to say that I took that hotdog to my wife without a single word. Even when I returned later with my own food and I saw that she had honored me by waiting to eat until I joined her, I remained silent and did not honor her in return by exchanging our hotdogs.

My heart was hard. I looked to find any excuse to justify my selfishness, and bury my conviction. I failed to consider the classic saying: "What would Jesus do?" Looking back, I cannot imagine him offering my wife a plate of dilapidated hotdogs while keeping the nicer ones for himself. In this small way, I refused to die for her as Christ died for me. Clearly no one's life was in danger in this story; nonetheless, I knew the right thing to do and didn't do it because of my own selfishness, just as James 4:17 warns.

Sadly, it wasn't until after the meal was over that I confessed my selfishness to my wife and asked her forgiveness. In that moment of clarity I realized that I needed a heart-level understanding of how, even in the smallest moments, a Christlike chivalrousness can guide my heart and behavior. Following Christ, we are called to die to ourselves. And this is not a command to solely lay down our physical bodies, but rather to die to our own self-serving pride:

Do nothing out of selfish ambition or vain conceit. Rather, in humility value others above yourselves, not looking to your own interests but each of you to the interests of the others. In your relationships with one another, have the same mindset as Christ Jesus: Who, being in very nature God, did not consider equality with God something to be used to his own advantage; rather, he made himself nothing by taking the very nature of a servant, being made in human likeness. And being found in appearance as a man, he humbled himself by becoming obedient to death-- even death on a cross!

- Philippians 2:3-8 NIV

What is that "same mindset" we are encouraged to have? Don't be selfish or conceited. Do be humble. Those parts are obvious. Jesus could have used his divinity to his advantage, but didn't. He took on the form of an obedient, mortal servant. Jesus is a living paradox. He died and rose to life. He is God, and he is man. He has total authority, and was totally obedient. He deserves the perfect hotdog, and takes the worst hotdog. And we are encouraged to emulate his mindset?! It seems impossible.

When we try to do so, we seem more likely to either demand the best or expect the worst because we have come to believe that that's what we deserve. We become either entitled or self-depreciating. I believe Jesus' mindset lies in the middle ground, where confidence and humility meet. Trying to discern just what defines that middleground has been debated for millenia. One of my favorite takes on which is chivalry.

What do you think of when you hear the word "chivalry"? Chivalry seems mysterious - like some ancient truth we've only half remembered. But I think it still evokes something deep within us. To me, the word evokes a mixture of thoughts, emotions, and responsibilities. Despite its common association, chivalry isn't just about how men treat women - it's about doing the right thing. And who doesn't imagine themselves doing what is right? Hence why chivalry, doing the right thing, resonates so deeply with us. Honor, heroism, and chivalry seem to be imprinted within us.

But of course there are those that dismiss chivalry, saying that it is either dead, a lie, or only an artifact of the past; that chivalry is merely a naive dream of our personal and societal immaturity. If anything, common forms of chivalry seem solely relegated to fiction. Pop culture fills our imaginations with whatever writers, producers, artists, and actors believe chivalry looks like. Typically this is portrayed as heroes in fantastical stories defeating impossible odds, falling in love, and saving the day. It is easy to see why so many dismiss chivalry when it only exists in fantasy and veiled history. Yet it clearly lingers on our minds, seemingly important, but eluding our efforts to pin down in our own lives.

Although historical accounts differ, the chivalric code was generally thought to be sworn by squires during their "ceremony of accolades," or knighting ceremony. A possible version of the ceremony of accolades, after the influence of Christianity on medieval Europe, involved an all-night prayer vigil the night before the ceremony with the squire clothed in white, and on the next morning came the ceremony itself. The squire would present himself to the royal court, his polished armor and sword lying on the altar behind his monarch. The squire would kneel before the altar, repeat the code of chivalry by memory and swear to uphold it, and would finally be christened a knight of the realm and presented with his sword and armor.

My favorite version of the code of chivalry survives from The Song of Roland, a thousand-year-old French poem which depicted the code, with 17 vows, as it was supposedly sworn by the knights of Charlemagne[5].

1. To fear God and maintain his Church
2. To serve the liege lord in valor and faith
3. To protect the weak and defenseless
4. To give aid to widows and orphans
5. To refrain from the wanton giving of offence
6. To live by honor and for glory
7. To despise monetary reward
8. To fight for the welfare of all
9. To obey those placed in authority
10. To guard the honor of fellow knights
11. To abstain from unfairness, meanness and deceit
12. To keep faith
13. At all times to speak the truth

14. To persevere to the end in any enterprise begun
15. To respect the honor of women
16. Never to refuse a challenge from an equal
17. Never to turn the back upon a foe

Chivalry is not some imposing moral achievement nor superpower to be used only in a time of crisis. It is a set of guidelines for daily living, ordinary life, and regular problems. Imagine the difference it would make if you saw something like this every morning on your way out of your room, or if you decided to memorize and then swear to the code of chivalry like an ancient knight. Would it cause you to think twice when you were about to lie, make a joke about your boss to a coworker, or serve a dilapidated hotdog to your spouse? In order to live a life grounded on a "good" foundation, we need reminders like the code of chivalry. Otherwise we're only guessing at life and making whatever move seems the most convenient or reasonable at the time.

Being heroic is an act we tell ourselves we would emulate if our lives mirrored that of the characters on movie screens. But our lives seem saturated not with epic, dramatic action and romance scenes, but with tiny moments where the results of our actions seem inconsequential. Like my story earlier about the hotdogs. We tell ourselves what we do won't matter. Why do the difficult, honorable thing when it produces little-to-no result? Why be the good guy if no one else is?

Now, most people will tell you that they want to be a good person, but who's to say what "good" is? "Good" seems easy to define in climactic moments of climactic, fictional conflict, where all the heroes are beautiful and the villains are horrifying. In books and movies, the stakes are massive. By comparison, discerning what it means to be good in our lives feels ambiguous and unimportant. Our lives seem dull.

This is my greatest pet peeve in life. That "normal life" is normal. That when you grow up, you "settle down." That life will be easy and good. That you'll live, "happily ever after."

There's a scene in Marvel's Avengers: Endgame[6] that perfectly captures how pervasive this ethos has become.

Sam, otherwise known as the Falcon, approaches an old man sitting on a bench. We see that it's Steve Rodgers, Captain America himself, but he's aged decades after traveling back in time.

"So did something go wrong, or something go right?" Sam asks.

Steve says he "tried some of that life," that Tony, Iron Man, told him to get. Although he doesn't tell Sam, the audience knows that Steve found the love of his life, Peggy, and spent his life with her.

"How'd that work out for you?" Sam asks.

Cap looks off into the distance. "It was beautiful," he replies.

The scene slows down, and the music swells.

"I'm happy for you," Sam says.

The movie so badly wants for this scene to be moving, but I just want to vomit. Now look, life can be beautiful. It can be breathtaking. Awe-inspiring. It can be simple and good. But that's not the whole story! There is nothing "normal" about "normal life." Everyone's story is touched by the trials of our flesh, our enemy, and our fallen world. Life is good, yes, but it is also heartbreaking. Expecting or portraying it to be anything different is a disservice to every single human being. When we live under this mentality, the adversity we will inevitably face becomes remarkably difficult to interpret:

Life must be all bad.

I was a fool for being so naive.

What's wrong with me?

Why is God punishing me?

How come it's so easy for everyone else?

I'm not cut out for this.

I never thought life would be so hard.

I won't ever look at things the same way again.

If I weren't such a failure, this wouldn't be a problem.

Thinking that ordinary life - whether it's going to school, finding a job, building a career, renting or owning a home, making friends, daily routines, dating and marriage, dealing with aging or illness, finding meaning in life, or raising a family - is *only* beautiful will hamstring us. The problems we run into, especially the ones that cannot be resolved quickly, will have us looking for escapism. Like watching a superhero movie. Bear with me: Why on Earth would we turn to media and stories *where the conflict is exaggerated?!* You'd think that for as difficult as life is, we'd bury ourselves in stories where everyone gets along and life is great. Let's all sing kumbaya. No, we crave drama. Why?

It's simple - sweeping, dramatic stories remind us that the conflicts we face in daily life are the ones that require the greatest courage. The hardest battles are not the ones fought on battlefields, they're the ones fought at home and in the heart. These stories remind us that we can overcome, or that it's at least worth trying. Strangely, counter-intuitively, unrealistic obstacles faced by humanistic characters help us to make sense of life.

Unfortunately, Captain America wasn't very human in his closing scene. The movie perpetuates the myth that life is easy. It could have been fixed so easily:

"How'd that work out for you?" Sam asks.

Cap turns, and looks at Sam. "It was the hardest thing I've ever done," he says. "And the best thing I've ever done."

This changes everything. All that Captain America has been through - Thanos and all the other challenges he faced - were all just a warm up to the real adventure. The superhero who faced down god-like enemies sees that ordinary people living ordinary lives require just as much strength, courage, and endurance. It's humbling. It's validating. It's encouraging. It means that "regular" life has meaning.

Ordinary life requires extraordinary courage.

When we really begin to grasp this reality things start to make more sense. The need to live life with honor starts to make sense. Life is full of trials and triumphs, to think that it is anything less is the actual fantasy. Oftentimes our battles are more related to maintaining this mindset than they are against the actual challenges themselves. In other words, it's easier to deal with a flat tire than it is to deal with our reactions to getting a flat tire. The goal of living honorably is not to avoid flat tires but to meet the moment with courage and Faith, which we can only accomplish when we see our lives for the adventures they are.

When we think our lives are drab, it's easy to justify our actions as "not that big of a deal." As soon as we fall victim to this mentality, we will multiply the damage done. We must recognize the small battles, and especially our reactions to those battles, for what they are: our greatest adversaries in life.

If we do not see life for the beauty *and* adversity that it is, there will be serious consequences. We will default to living comfortably, and react indignantly to anyone or anything that disturbs us. Others' rebukes towards us will seem like overly-sensitive criticism, disposing us to minimize their legitimate complaints. We will become more prone to justify ourselves, finding excuses to nullify the pain we inflict on others. We turn passive and stubborn, quick to assign blame and fault. We become arrogant and refuse to apologize or take responsibility. This is someone who might say, "I did nothing wrong," and constantly finds fault with others. But justification can take another form, which seems entirely opposite. When we believe that problems in life are the product of our own failures, we turn to false humility. This is the mindset of someone who says, "I can't do anything right," and blames themselves for being a failure. Both mindsets refuse to acknowledge the battle that life really is, and as a result, both fail to meet life's challenges.

Living between arrogance and self-deprecation means that when we make a mistake we neither blame our circumstances, others, nor ourselves. Instead, we are able to be honest about our faults, whatever they may be, and also be honest about our capability of doing better. This, I think, is true honor. It's not about perfection, but improvement. And not improvement because of fear, but because of Faith. Honor is not a goal, it's a means of living. While it is important to have goals, they are insufficient to keep us going through all the difficulty we will encounter in life. While we strive for Faith, we will contend with the lure to give in to Manipulation, Greed, and Apathy. We will fail on some level to live in accordance with all that we have vowed or want to be. Even as we attempt to love others with God's love, our character is disparate from God's perfect nature.

Earlier this year, I was driving into work when I saw a highway worker cutting grass beside the freeway. I thought about what it must be like to live in this man's shoes, and wondered how he felt about his work, cutting grass. Does he love his job, or despise it? If he cuts grass only because of the satisfaction he receives after he mows a perfectly manicured lawn, then he must be miserable. Grass grows back day after day, year after year. There is no permanency in the fruit of his labor. After cutting one patch of grass, it's on to the next one, and back a week later to do it all over again.

If we pursue some objective, however admirable, because we hate the state of imperfection, happiness will elude us. We either spend our lives miserable or give up. On the other hand, if we can find fulfillment in the process, then we can continue on and be well. If our satisfaction is not only derived from a nice lawn, but also from the process of mowing itself, then our lives become rich. There's a quote from Albert Einstein that perfectly captures this dilemma:

A calm and modest life brings more happiness than the pursuit of success combined with constant restlessness.

- Albert Einstein

Just like the highway worker with his grass, we must not improve ourselves out of distaste for our imperfections. Rather, it is the process of growing, maturing, and improving that we must come to savor. Proverbs 12:1 (NIV) doesn't pull any punches when it comes to the importance of appreciating self growth.

"Whoever loves discipline loves knowledge, but whoever hates correction is stupid."

Please hear this: we so often have "correction" or "discipline" that is done poorly, which causes us to fear making mistakes. Proverbs 12:1 itself almost becomes self-defeating, teetering on the edge of a rebuke too harsh to swallow. When we are rebuffed with cruelty, mockery, or derision, we learn to fear correction and thus become trapped in a lifestyle where we *must* be perfect. This hardens our heart to the point where we cannot hear gentle corrections and write off harsh rebukes as asinine.

In order to love discipline, we must be treated with wisdom and kindness when we make mistakes. Hint: no one is. People or circumstances will eventually come around that will kick us while we're down. And so we learn to fear mistakes to avoid being shamed. We cannot live honorably, seeing daily life for the battle that it is, while we are paralyzed and blinded by pain and fear. If so, failures, setbacks, and disappointments will take us out. The secret of honor is the ability to make mistakes, learn from them, and grow. Honor isn't about doing what is right, it's about admitting when you've done wrong and then committing yourself to doing better. But our past hurts can keep us from valuing our missteps. To break free, we need to be healed from, and overcome, the messages we've internalized over the years. We need God to meet us where we fall.

Healing and Overcoming

Once upon a time a young girl, who we'll call Susie, wanted to play softball with her friends. Susie had watched a high school game recently, and instantly fell in love with the sport. Convincing her friends took some work, but eventually she got them all to agree to play. Her parents took her to the store, and they bought softballs, gloves, and a bat for her and her friends to use. They drove to a field, and her friends arrived. They split into teams, and her team was first up to bat. A few girls went before her, then finally, it was her turn. She got up to the plate and readied herself.

The pitch came in low, and it hit the ground several feet in front of her. But, being eager, she swung hard at it, but missed. Several of the girls in the infield chuckled. Susie steeled her resolve, and dug in for the next pitch. This one came in fast - too fast - and she didn't swing. A strike. Frustrated with herself, and trying to tune out the heckling from the other team, she tightened her grip and waited for the third pitch.

The ball came in looking good, and she swung as hard as she could. She closed her eyes, expecting the crack of the bat, but it never came. Instead, the bat slipped from her hands, and went flying end over end into the infield. The sudden change in weight knocked her off balance. She spun around and fell. Looking up, she saw the other team in a fit of laughter. Worse, Susie's own team was laughing and pointing at her. Someone started calling her "Swinging Susie," and other names followed. Shame heated her cheeks and tears fell from her eyes.

She spent the rest of the game in the dug-out, and vowed to never play again.

Years later, when she was in college, some of her new friends invited Susie to play in a softball recreational team for fun. The nearly forgotten memories of her friends' laughter and name calling suddenly came back to her, and she found herself unable to speak. After all that had happened and all that time, there was still a part of her that wanted to play. But there was another part that paralyzed her, warning her that no good would come of it.

Opening our hearts to receive the goodness we yearn for takes courage after we've been hurt. We fear that it's going to be the same old thing all over again. That it's somehow a trick - that there's going to be another shoe that drops, or that the rug will be pulled out from underneath us. We look our gift horses in the mouth not because we're ungrateful, but because life has taught us to be suspicious. Goodness becomes a trigger for anxiety. And it's not just the original goodness where we first encountered harm that we've learned to mistrust, but also the goodness of healing. So we close ourselves off instead. But all the while we hold out a tentative hope. We want someone to skirt our defenses, dodge every boobytrap we've set around our hearts, and convince us that it's safe to receive goodness once again.

We want someone to earn our trust while we sit back and watch. It should go without saying that no human being can possibly do enough to deserve the de-armament of our defenses. We need Christ, our savior, to rescue us out of the hurt and defensiveness we find ourselves in. However, in our defensive posture, expect him on *our* terms. But God doesn't always conform to our whims. This does not mean that we will be left to suffer the fate of our own crushing, self-protective measures, though. God finds ways to meet us that are both far easier, and far more difficult, than we might dare imagine.

First, we've got to talk about our walls - the things we do that we think keep us from being hurt again. Our walls cause us to avoid any possible triggers, any situations similar to the original incident of harm. For instance, Susie might refuse to play in the rec league even though she is now with an entirely different group of people. Perhaps she even has full confidence that these people are kind and gentle. But her defenses have already dictated: softball = bad. If we allow these kinds of inhibiting walls to keep us safe indefinitely, they will grow. Putting up walls might help for a time, but eventually the fear we harbor becomes reinforced. We teach ourselves that fear is what helps us to feel secure, so the more we desire security the more we will live in fear.

While we self-protect, we believe that our walls keep others out. And indeed, they do. Therefore we come to believe that we are alone in our pain, that we have hedged ourselves in. While this strategy might keep others from seeing our wounds or hurting us again, it doesn't keep out God. God doesn't need to dismantle our defenses, *because he's already behind our walls.* We're so busy keeping others out that we pay no mind to what is happening inside our very walls.

I pray that out of his glorious riches he may strengthen you with power through his Spirit in your inner being, so that Christ may dwell in your hearts through faith.

- Ephesians 3:16-17 NIV

Our avoidance, denial, and posturing doesn't keep God out. He knows the difference between when we're well and only pretending to be well, because he dwells in our innermost being. Our walls might keep some people from seeing our hurts, but God sees and knows. And thank God for that. His intimacy with us where we are most wounded gives us a lifeline to hold onto. We can have confidence that even though our lives might not go as we want, we always have Jesus. He loves us in our darkest hours. God is able to meet us wherever we are. Our walls do not stop Jesus from knowing, loving, and healing us.

For a time, there is nothing wrong with putting up some walls towards the things that hurt you. Maybe it's time to reconsider who your friends really are, or whether it's really worth it to continue the sport you've been playing. Having some healthy boundaries is essential to life. We cannot heal if we're continuing to be hurt. After we've put up some walls, it's ripe timing to pursue healing. Healing doesn't require us to deal with the things that hurt us, only that we deal with the actual hurt itself. So long as we are mindful about it, it's okay to have walls and to find healing. There's a big difference between reactive and proactive mechanisms for healing. If we only react, we might try to numb ourselves with poor coping mechanisms that leave us in worse shape. However, if we carefully consider how to go about finding healing, we will find we have a treasure-trove of resources.

There are opportunities all around us to deal with our hurt. Even deciding to stop and notice something good for a few seconds is enough to offer you a dose of healing. It might be a gentle breeze, a sunset, or your favorite song. These opportunities for healing are easy to ignore but immensely rejuvenating when we pay them mind. Healing refuels us to engage life as it comes by opening us up to the small gifts of God's goodness we so often miss.

When we encounter awesome beauty in creation - a new baby, a thunderous waterfall, a sweeping canyon, or moving artwork - we seem more likely to take pictures than we are to really be present to and savor the moment. We are meant to live our lives as God's beloved, not as tourists. This doesn't mean you can't take pictures, only that we must be willing to receive, and that means giving the moment our attention.

Ralph Waldo Emerson writes in *Nature and Selected Essays*[7]:

"If the stars should appear one night in a thousand years, how would men believe and adore; and preserve for many generations the remembrance of the city of God which had been shown! But every night come out these envoys of beauty, and light the universe with their admonishing smile. (...) To speak truly, few adult persons can see nature. Most persons do not see the sun. At least they have a very superficial seeing. The sun illuminates only the eye of the man, but shines into the eye and the heart of the child. The lover of nature is he whose inward and outward senses are still truly adjusted to each other; who has retained the spirit of infancy even into the era of manhood."

Instead of being captivated by the stars, we go about our business with little regard to the beauty that dances around us. We miss small moments like this all the time. It is easy to get desensitized and numb to small gestures of beauty, especially if life comes to us pre-tailored and barbless (as it does in the so-called "American Dream"). We have to retrain ourselves to be aware of goodness. A quiet evening at home after a hectic day, the comfort of a warm shower, and the faces of your loved ones are all packed with the holiness, beauty, and healing touch of God. Keeping an open heart and alert mind ("the spirit of infancy") draws us to be attentive to even the smallest forms of goodness we usually pay no attention to.

Pausing to appreciate goodness, especially in the midst of pain or turmoil, is one of the most courageous acts we can do. It is not denial, where we refuse to acknowledge difficulty, but a proclamation of truth: that goodness is greater than evil. Through awareness and appreciation of small moments of goodness, we cultivate a recognition of God's presence despite our momentary circumstances. God becomes our safe place, and that knowledge allows us to navigate the fray. Good triumphs over evil when we delight ourselves in God during our darkest hours. In allowing for joy, we teach others (and our own stubborn hearts) about the goodness, peace, and healing that await us in the arms of Christ.

But we need more than just healing. Though our walls might help us to heal from damage that has been done to us, our walls do nothing to help us live freely.

For example, let's say you sprained your ankle. While at first you need to use the "RICE" acronym: Rest, Ice, Compression, and Elevation, eventually you have to change strategies. But that change is difficult. You want to walk, but you don't want to deal with the pain of your ankle. It doesn't hurt so bad when you've got it propped up on the couch, though. So there you stay, long past the time when resting was beneficial. Now it has become avoidant. What was once necessary for your healing is now atrophying you. When others say that you've rested long enough, and it's time to start moving again, you protest. You claim RICE as your justification. You say that you're doing your best, that your ankle is healing by you leaving it alone, and that time heals all wounds. But the truth is, for as badly as you might want to walk, the pain of your injury and fear of getting hurt again has become more important. The longer you sit, the more your ankle withers. If you do try to walk, now it only hurts worse, which confirms your fears and keeps you off your feet even longer.

Similarly, when our defenses ensnare us, turning to our old places of comfort can do more harm than good. Healing is a balm to the human heart and body, true. But if you break your leg, the cast isn't meant to stay on forever. Eventually we outgrow our supports, and after that point, leaning on them will only cripple us further. Healing is meant to usher us into freedom, not keep us overly dependent.

This is not to say that we cannot learn from our experiences and have better boundaries and self-governance. Obviously, it does us no good if we are wounded and repeat the exact same actions, expecting things to be different. We need wisdom to know the difference between the situations that harm us and those that are safe. If we don't, we'll project our hurt onto anything that bears even a remote similarity to our triggers. That fear will continue to multiply until it completely ensnares us.

If softball is better off avoided, then perhaps all sports should be avoided. If sports are dangerous, then anything competitive is dangerous. If competition is dangerous, then social situations are dangerous. Since social situations are dangerous, people should be avoided. Before we know it we find ourselves living in crippling fear and isolation.

If we were only interested in healing (not feeling pain) we would never do anything remotely risky ever again. But to live abundantly, not just comfortably, we need to be able to take some risks in life. We must be able to lower our guard, open our gates and lower our drawbridges. Otherwise, we won't be able to receive anything good. We'll live our lives suspicious, and we won't let love in.

Healing only grants us an alleviation of pain. Living our lives avoiding all pain, however, is folly. If we're not careful, fear will quickly step in to keep us "safe." Living in fearful safety where the world is always 100% predictable is soul-killing. There must come a time when we are ready to stake actual risks in order to find real rewards.

There is no way to receive anything good when we refuse to let anyone or anything in. Eventually our walls must be re-examined. But first we have to recognize that our walls are trapping us, which is remarkably hard to accept. When others point out this problem to us, it is rarely done with the kindness, honesty, and wisdom we so desperately need. Even when done well, it can be exposing, embarrassing, and immensely frustrating. Although we cannot afford to continue hiding behind our walls once we know we're being stifled by them, denying the problem and thinking that everyone else must be wrong feels easier.

Gaining awareness of this problem doesn't feel like healing, because it isn't. Healing soothes and comforts; bringing our walls down is uncomfortable, yet necessary. I like to call this act "overcoming." Overcoming is the act of confronting and adjusting our walls, together with God's love and prompting. Healing is freedom from pain. Overcoming is freedom from fear.

Overcoming is a *result* of healing, not a part of the healing process itself. This is a critical distinction, as we will do harm when we expect ourselves or others to overcome when we haven't fully healed. And, even though we might be working to overcome our past hurts, that doesn't mean we cannot return to our place of healing when needed. In fact, being able to do so is crucial to have the courage necessary to overcome. Then, as we're ready, we reach out again and again.

Scary as that might sound, there's some good news. We often stay trapped behind our defenses because we fear something unrealistic: that once we let one of our walls down, they will all come crashing down like dominos. Thankfully, God doesn't bulldoze our walls down. If so, we would have no say in the matter, and our growth would be meaningless. While overcoming isn't as out of control as we fear, it still requires our participation and courage. For Susie, it might mean taking her friends up on their invitation or even simply asking if she can come watch a game before signing up.

We do not have to rush it. Trying to push ourselves for more than what we're ready for is cruelty. Rather, when we have experienced healing it opens the door for the opportunity to exchange our walls for drawbridges. We need the assurance of knowing that we can return to our places of healing if lowering our walls goes poorly; that we don't have to continue if it's too hard. There is no punishment, no judgment, no condemnation if we say we're not ready. We can take our time. We're not expected to completely rid ourselves of the ways we've learned to stay safe. Overcoming only means that we incidentally re-examine where our means of safety have become prohibitive of the desires of our hearts. But we cannot do this work on others' terms. When we look back on the small, courageous choices we made to overcome, we need to know that it was our choice - not someone else's. That way we know our growth is legitimate. When we decide we're ready, when it is *our* decision, then we overcome.

If we've let in a Trojan Horse in our past, how are we to open our gates again? How do we know if we're ready to take the risk when someone wheels up another "gift?" It's not realistic to expect ourselves to feel fully confident without a shadow of doubt. As such, we cannot gauge our readiness based solely on how we feel. Now, while clichés come to mind, such as "you'll know when you're ready," or "ask God to show you," I think we can do more. We know that we're ready to lower our drawbridges when we've accepted the chance that the outcome could be exactly what we're afraid of, but still worth the risk. In essence, this means that we have reconciled the inner tension between what we are afraid of, and what we desire. We are able to look both squarely in the eyes and take action in line with what we value most. In this sense, negative outcomes are more easily interpreted as worthwhile obstacles to obtaining our objectives. "Failure" becomes manageable.

Our walls become more flexible when we decide that we're okay with failure - that we would be okay and willing to try again in the future. This readiness may come as we recognize that the potential positive outcomes outweigh the potential negatives. And, should the outcome be negative, we feel prepared to deal with it. Most importantly, we focus on the courage and growth we gain as we confront our fears with God - not on the outcome itself. We find the courage to come out from behind our walls because of the confidence we have in God. At any time, we can return to him for a place of sheltering safety and venture out again when we're ready. Life cannot be about avoiding pain, but rather must be about what pain we decide is worth it.

About a month ago, I raised my four-year-old's training wheels on his bicycle. I explained to him that he was getting better at pedaling, and that it was time to start learning a bit of balance. He helped me get out my wrenches and raise each side by about a half inch. He was excited until he saw, standing beside his bike, that it now had a slight wobble.

Suddenly, he was screaming and crying. "Change it back! Change it back! Nooooo! I don't like it!"

I tried to console him, and told him that it was going to be okay. But he was having none of it. "I don't want to ride my bike. Noooo! Change it back!"

"But it'll help you to have more traction and to go faster," I reasoned.

"I don't like it!" he cried.

Not wanting to force him to do something he clearly didn't feel ready for, I thought about how to make sense of the situation.

"You don't like that I raised your training wheels?" I asked.

"No! Change it back, daddy!"

"Is it because you don't like that it wobbles?"

"Yes! I don't like the wobble!" He said through tears.

"Is it scary to you?"

"Yes!"

"Does it make you afraid that you are going to fall over?"

"Yeeeeees!"

"Yeah, you're scared you're going to fall over because it feels wobbly now. Well, I'll walk right beside you, buddy. I'll make sure you don't fall over," I told him.

"No! Just change it back!"

I thought for a moment. "How about this," I said. "Let's ride your bike to the end of the street and back. I'll help hold onto your bike so it won't fall over. And, if you still don't like it when we get back, I'll put your training wheels back down."

He sniffled, and looked between me and his bike. "Okay," he said hesitantly.

So, I helped him onto his bicycle and we slowly started making our way down the road. It definitely was more wobbly, as he feared, but I was there to keep him from tipping over.

"See, I've got you," I said. "It is more wobbly now, but you're not falling over. When you go faster, your bike won't wobble as much too."

I felt proud of him for trying something scary, and for trusting me to keep him safe. Mainly, I was proud of him for making the decision to give it a try. He wasn't forced into riding his bike, nor was he chastised for being afraid and crying. I was happy to reward his courage by reverting his training wheels back to where he felt more safe when we returned.

Except, I didn't need to.

We weren't more than a dozen steps down the road when he exclaimed, "Let go, dad! I want to go fast! I'm not scared anymore!"

And then he was off, zipping down the road like it was nothing. I was completely dumbfounded. I had entirely expected to guide him the whole way, then revert his training wheels as he wanted.

Instead, he practiced turning on his own and quickly acclimated to the wobble. In fact, he drove his bike into our grass and fell over on purpose. Then popped his head up and shouted, "I'm okay!" In the blink of an eye he was back on his bike and I had to shout for him to wait up for me!

I'm not a perfect parent. No one is. I have my own moments where I scream and cry out to God in fear and frustration. I make mistakes. But thankfully, God *is* the perfect parent. He is our comforter and counselor. Yet, God is also the most unpredictable, uncontrollable entity we can ever come into contact with. But he is also the most familiar. Because of who he is, God alone has the capacity to bring us out of our restrictive comfort zones while also meeting us exactly wherever we are.

Like he did with Peter, God takes us to the ends of our Faith. When situations seem hopeless, when our ability to trust God is pushed to its limit, God breaks through in breathtaking vibrancy. He shows us, time and again, that his goodness is the final word. God's faithfulness fundamentally changes and heals us; it allows us to overcome. It restructures our defenses from the inside-out and the outside-in, eventually leading us to a place of safety we might have never thought possible.

There are three kinds of safety. We first feel a sense of safety when we are innocent and therefore ignorant of the dangers surrounding us. But, because we cannot see the danger, we also cannot see our own nakedness. Innocence is bliss, as they say.

But then our innocence is broken and we see the dangers we were blind to. To find safety now, we become self-protective and hypervigilant. We curse our nakedness and seek to arm ourselves to the teeth. We put up defenses of every kind: we place blame, analyze every past and future situation, we use denial and avoidance, and give into resignation and bitterness. All of these strategies are merely misplaced attempts to return to that place of blissful innocence - to unsee what has been seen. But we cannot forget. Self-protection might limit pain, but it certainly is haunted by the memory of pain. This kind of "safety" is a poor alternative to the safety God offers.

Through healing and overcoming, we arrive to the final place of safety: wisdom. With immense kindness and careful pruning, God removes all the defenses we erroneously think keep us safe. Wisdom does not leave us defenseless nor does it trap us in overprotection. Wisdom allows us to appropriately discern between when to be vulnerable and when to be guarded. With wisdom, we can do something that neither innocence nor self-protection ever could. We can choose to take on danger for the right reasons (which self-protection could never do), and accept goodness with careful consideration (which innocence could never do). Wisdom allows us to see the goodness in adversity and the adversity in goodness.

This process grants us a deep, abiding contentment, independent of whether events transpire favorably or not, and not because we are cynical or in denial. The contentment of wisdom comes from a profound truth, which Thucydides wrote about in his account of the *History of the Peloponnesian War:*

> *"The bravest are surely those who have the clearest vision of what is before them, glory and danger alike, and yet notwithstanding, go out to meet it."* and *"The secret of happiness is freedom and the secret of freedom is courage."*

We desire glory, yes, but how often do we find ourselves trapped by the fear of danger? When we recognize how unpredictable life can be, it's easy to feel like disappointment is inevitable. However, in God we find that we are not helpless. We do not have perfect wisdom in discerning how the courses we choose in life will end. When trouble happens we can either refuse to accept it and waste time fighting reality, or acknowledge the pain and begin to work on what we actually have control over - ourselves. When we do so, we are awakened to the hurts that we've harbored, the disappointments we've suffered, and our terrifying lack of control. But we also find healing and meaning in our pain.

God meets us in our wounded places, kissing our tears and holding us tight. In God's overwhelming love, our agony subsides. Our hope is restored. Then, bit by bit, he walks with us as we journey out from under the burden of our wounds. He gently leads us in the pathway he modeled for us. We find the freedom to take risks and accept difficulty because we see adversity as the pathway we chose, not something thrust upon us. The journey brings us closer to our ultimate goal - intimacy with God, and wholeness with ourselves. We are re-established in our capacity to have faith, hope, and love.

Living in faith, hope, and love is the antithesis to the sinful power of Manipulation, Greed, and Apathy. Faith disarms the insecurity that drives us to Manipulation, empowering us to rest in trust rather than futility grasping for control. Hope draws us to long for the goodness of God as opposed to the fleeting pleasures we might seek on our own. Lust does not abide hope, but seeks to numb it. Hope reawakens our God-given desires and creates dissatisfaction for anything less. And finally, love keeps us safe from Apathy. When we feel defeated and like giving up, God's love buoys us. God never stops fighting for us, even when we tell ourselves we've stopped caring.

We are shaped by the forces that put pressure on us. Adversity molds us. Evil attempts to harm us. We all, by nature and to varying degrees, conform to the pressures surrounding us. Harshness begets resentment. Selfishness, disgust. Abandonment, fear. Powerlessness, hopelessness. But love begets love. Tasting God's goodness and love spurs us to love him in return, honoring him with our lives. And what is God honored by? Not by perfect people, nor by thoughtless gifts. God is honored by daughters and sons so captivated by his love that they seek to emulate him. We emulate him not for our own pride, but to sidle up closer to God's heart.

Our hope is that despite adversity to any extent or severity, that the loving pressure of God is the ultimate crucible, far greater than any trial. God's beauty and power heal us. And in the molding and healing, there is growth. We are changed. We overcome. God holds his hand out to us, ready to walk with us through all the beauty and pain. We find the strength to do so in Christ, who went ahead before us and forged the pathway to Faith.

Scripture: *I have learned to be content whatever the circumstances. I know what it is to be in need, and I know what it is to have plenty. I have learned the secret of being content in any and every situation, whether well fed or hungry, whether living in plenty or in want. I can do all this through him who gives me strength. - Philippians 4:11-13 NIV*

Thought: Misfortunes serve the hopeful not as haunting memories, but revered markers along the pathways of our life walked together with God.

Questions:

- How do you know that God is good when he doesn't do what you want him to do?
- When life doesn't go the way that you want it to, how do you distinguish what is in your control from what is not?
- How do you see yourself when you make a mistake?
- What's one of your walls God is inviting to you re-examine?

Notes

Chapter 1

1   Williams, R. (2005). *The truce of God: Peacemaking in troubled times* (pp. 90-91). Norwich: Canterbury Press.
2   Crabb, L., Hudson, D., & Andrews, A. (2013). *Men of courage: God's call to move beyond the silence of Adam*. Grand Rapids, MI: Zondervan.

Chapter 2

1   Shedd, J. A. (1928). *Salt from my attic*. Portland, ME: Mosher Press.
2   Crabb, Hudson, Andrews, *Men of courage*

Chapter 3

1   Evans, R. L. (1976). *Richard Evans' quote book*. Salt Lake City, UT: Press.
2   Rotter, Julian B (1966). "Generalized expectancies for internal versus external control of reinforcement". Psychological Monographs: General and Applied. 80 (1): 1–28. doi:10.1037/h0092976
3.   Frankl, F. (2006). *Man's Search for Meaning*. Beacon Press.

Chapter 5

1   Webster, J. (1912). *Daddy Long Legs*. New York, NY: Grosset & Dunlap.

Chapter 6

1   Sanders, C., & DeBlois, D. (Directors). (2010). *How to Train Your Dragon* [Motion picture]. United States: DreamWorks Animation; Paramount Pictures.
2   Sanderson, B. (2017). *Oathbringer*. New York, NY: Tor Books.

3   Seligman, M. E. P. (1972). "Learned helplessness". *Annual Review of Medicine.* 23 (1): 407–412. doi:10.1146/annurev.me.23.020172.002203.

4   Marcus Aurelius, *Meditations*. IV. 49, trans. Hicks

5   Code of Chivalry. (2018, March). Retrieved 2021, from http://www.medieval-life-and-times.info/medieval-knights/code-of-chivalry.htm

6   Russo, A., & Russo, J. (Directors). (2019). *Avengers: Endgame* [Motion picture]. United States: Marvel Studios; Walt Disney Studios Motion Pictures.

7   Emerson, R. W., & Ziff, L. (2003). *Nature and selected essays*. Penguin Books.